王荣华／译注

千字文

双语版

THE VERSE OF ONE THOUSAND CHARACTERS

English-Chinese Edition

Translated, with Annotations by
WANG RONGHUA

中国人民大学出版社
·北京·

Preface 前言

The Verse of One Thousand Characters is the oldest enlightenment textbook in China. It came into being earlier than the other enlightenment textbooks such as *The Three-Character a Line Chant* and *Family Names in Hundreds*. It has been used as a primer to teach children characters. We know for sure who the poet was and when it was composed. We don't have definite knowledge of who the authors were of the *Three* and the *Hundred* and when they were written. Some people refer to it as "One Thousand Character Classic". Even though it has been in existence for over 15 centuries and its readership is the biggest, it is not proper to regard it as a "classic".

《千字文》是中国最早的启蒙读物。它的问世要早于《三字经》和《百家姓》。它是用来教孩子们认字的。我们知道其作者是谁以及创作的时间。至于"三"和"百"是谁写的，何时写成，我们了解得并不确切。有人在英文里将《千字文》称为"经"。尽管它已存世 15 个世纪之久，并且其读者是最多的，但是称其为"经"还是不合适的。

The reasons for the author to give a paraphrase of the *Verse* are the following: firstly, it tells us what the most important one thousand characters are for the Chinese people. The *Verse* was intended to teach children how to write in the past 15 centuries. The one thousand characters were chosen by Yin Tieshi（殷铁石），a literary assistant in the imperial court of the Southern Dynasty, on orders of Emperor Wu of Liang（梁武帝，464 - 549），for children of the royal family to learn.

笔者之所以要译注这本书，原因如下：第一，它告诉我们中国人首先要认识的最重要的一千个字有哪些。在过去的 15 个世纪里，这本书主要用来教孩子们认字。这些字最初是由南朝皇宫里的文学侍从殷铁石，按照梁武帝（464—549）的旨意，为了教皇家儿童认字找出来的。

However, these characters were not related to each other and it was difficult for children to remember. The Emperor then asked Zhou Xingsi（周兴嗣）to piece these characters together. Zhou was at that time a middle ranking officer among the retinue of advisors on horse-backs when the emperor was on a tour. It took Zhou only one night to render the one thousand characters into a four-character-a-line verse. The next day, when the Emperor read it, he was amazingly surprised and ordered to have it printed. Since then, the *Verse* has been on the lips of Chinese people for over 1,500 years.

但是，这一千个字相互不关联，记忆起来很困难。于是，梁武帝命周兴嗣将这一千个字组织成一篇诗文。彼时，周兴嗣任员外散骑侍郎，是个中级官员。他只用了一个晚上就将这一千个字编成了四字一行的诗文。次日，梁武帝读了千字文，十分惊喜，立即命人去印刷。从那时起，在1 500多年的时间里，它成了中国人一直诵读的名篇。

Secondly, it tells what the most important things children should know and learn. The one thousand characters cover such aspects as astronomy, nature, self-cultivation, ethics, morality, geography, history, farming, gardening, rituals and daily life. Zhou was not in good health. He suffered from eczema, and was once infected with malaria and one of his eyes lost sight. Ren Fang（任昉），one of his colleagues exclaimed that Zhou would have been appointed a vice minister of the Procuratorial Supervision in a matter of ten days if only he were in good health.

第二，它告诉我们儿童应该了解和学习的重要知识。这一千个字所涉及的内容有天文、自然、自我修养、伦理、道德、地理、历史、农耕、花圃、祭祀和日常生活。周兴嗣那时身体不好，患有湿疹，且感染过疟疾，有一只眼睛还失明了。他的同僚任昉感叹道："周兴嗣如果没病，十天内就能当上御史中丞。"

The *Verse* can thus serve as a key to Chinese traditional culture. It is the best enlightenment textbook in China and marks the highest level in the rudimentary phase in China's traditional education. It is a long poem in four lines and a mini encyclopedia of China.

这篇诗文可作打开中国传统文化的钥匙。它是中国最好的启蒙读物，标志着中国传统教育中初级阶段的最高水平。它既是一首四言长诗，又是一部简要的中国百科全书。

Even though the characters may look strange for those who haven't learned the Chinese language, they can still be able to see how the verse sounds and rhymes through "pin yin" (pronunciation in Chinese phonetic alphabet); they can still find out meanings in each line. Of course, for those who have been learning the Chinese language, this paper could assist them in getting a deeper understanding of these one thousand characters.

对于没有学习过汉语的人来说,这一千个字看起来很怪。但是,由于使用了汉语拼音标注,他们仍可以知道这些字怎么读,如何押韵;仍可以了解每行字是什么意思。当然,对于已经学习了一些汉语的人来说,这篇诗文可以帮助他们更深入地了解这一千个字。

The importance of this verse can be seen from the fact that quite a number of most influential calligraphers in Chinese history had written down this verse with their brush pens in various scripts, and the texts of these precious calligraphy are still available today. Ever since the heat wave of "China Studies" has been surged in China, more and more Chinese are reading and learning this verse.

中国历史上很多有影响的书法家都以各种书体写过《千字文》,可见其重要性。这些书法家的真迹仍被保留和收藏。国学热在中国兴起后,越来越多的人开始学习这篇诗文。

The way of paraphrasing is done in such an order: the characters will be listed line by line, and then the "pinyin" will be followed, and then a literal translation of the line with some notes and explanations of some characters. In the end, a polished version of the translation is presented.

笔者的译注顺序是这样的：先列出一行一行的汉字；然后给出字的汉语拼音；之后，给出此行文字的意译，并对有些字给出注释；最后，再给出修饰过的全篇英文诗文。

目录

The Verse of One Thousand Characters 千字文

1. Line 1　　天地玄黄 / 1
2. Line 2　　宇宙洪荒 / 2
3. Line 3　　日月盈昃 / 3
4. Line 4　　辰宿列张 / 4
5. Line 5　　寒来暑往 / 5
6. Line 6　　秋收冬藏 / 6
7. Line 7　　闰余成岁 / 7
8. Line 8　　律吕调阳 / 8
9. Lines 9 & 10　　云腾致雨，露结为霜 / 9
10. Lines 11 & 12　　金生丽水，玉出昆冈 / 10
11. Lines 13 & 14　　剑号巨阙，珠称夜光 / 11
12. Lines 15 & 16　　果珍李柰，菜重芥姜 / 12
13. Lines 17 & 18　　海咸河淡，鳞潜羽翔 / 13

14. Lines 19 & 20　龙师火帝，鸟官人皇 / 13
15. Lines 21 & 22　始制文字，乃服衣裳 / 15
16. Lines 23 & 24　推位让国，有虞陶唐 / 16
17. Lines 25 & 26　吊民伐罪，周发殷汤 / 17
18. Lines 27 & 28　坐朝问道，垂拱平章 / 18
19. Lines 29 & 30　爱育黎首，臣伏戎羌 / 18
20. Lines 31 & 32　遐迩一体，率宾归王 / 19
21. Lines 33 & 34　鸣凤在竹，白驹食场 / 19
22. Lines 35 & 36　化被草木，赖及万方 / 20
23. Lines 37 & 38　盖此身发，四大五常 / 21
24. Lines 39 & 40　恭惟鞠养，岂敢毁伤 / 21
25. Lines 41 & 42　女慕贞洁，男效才良 / 23
26. Lines 43 & 44　知过必改，得能莫忘 / 23
27. Lines 45 & 46　罔谈彼短，靡恃己长 / 24
28. Lines 47 & 48　信使可覆，器欲难量 / 25
29. Lines 49 & 50　墨悲丝染，诗赞羔羊 / 25
30. Lines 51 & 52　景行维贤，克念作圣 / 26
31. Lines 53 & 54　德建名立，形端表正 / 27
32. Lines 55 & 56　空谷传声，虚堂习听 / 27
33. Lines 57 & 58　祸因恶积，福缘善庆 / 28
34. Lines 59 & 60　尺璧非宝，寸阴是竞 / 28
35. Lines 61 & 62　资父事君，曰严与敬 / 29

36. Lines 63 & 64　孝当竭力，忠则尽命 / 30

37. Lines 65 & 66　临深履薄，夙兴温凊 / 31

38. Lines 67 & 68　似兰斯馨，如松之盛 / 32

39. Lines 69 & 70　川流不息，渊澄取映 / 33

40. Lines 71 & 72　容止若思，言辞安定 / 33

41. Lines 73 & 74　笃初诚美，慎终宜令 / 34

42. Lines 75 & 76　荣业所基，籍甚无竟 / 35

43. Lines 77 & 78　学优登仕，摄职从政 / 35

44. Lines 79 & 80　存以甘棠，去而益咏 / 37

45. Line 81　乐殊贵贱 / 38

46. Line 82　礼别尊卑 / 39

47. Lines 83 & 84　上和下睦，夫唱妇随 / 40

48. Lines 85 & 86　外受傅训，入奉母仪 / 40

49. Lines 87 & 88　诸姑伯叔，犹子比儿 / 41

50. Lines 89 & 90　孔怀兄弟，同气连枝 / 42

51. Lines 91 & 92　交友投分，切磨箴规 / 43

52. Lines 93 & 94　仁慈隐恻，造次弗离 / 43

53. Lines 95 & 96　节义廉退，颠沛匪亏 / 44

54. Lines 97 & 98　性静情逸，心动神疲 / 45

55. Lines 99 & 100　守真志满，逐物意移 / 45

56. Lines 101 & 102　坚持雅操，好爵自縻 / 46

57. Lines 103 & 104　都邑华夏，东西二京 / 46

3

58. Lines 105 & 106　背邙面洛，浮渭据泾 / 47
59. Lines 107 & 108　宫殿盘郁，楼观飞惊 / 48
60. Lines 109 & 110　图写禽兽，画彩仙灵 / 49
61. Lines 111 & 112　丙舍傍启，甲帐对楹 / 49
62. Lines 113 & 114　肆筵设席，鼓瑟吹笙 / 50
63. Lines 115 & 116　升阶纳陛，弁转疑星 / 50
64. Lines 117 & 118　右通广内，左达承明 / 51
65. Lines 119 & 120　既集坟典，亦聚群英 / 52
66. Lines 121 & 122　杜稿钟隶，漆书壁经 / 53
67. Lines 123 & 124　府罗将相，路侠槐卿 / 54
68. Lines 125 & 126　户封八县，家给千兵 / 55
69. Lines 127 & 128　高冠陪辇，驱毂振缨 / 56
70. Lines 129 & 130　世禄侈富，车驾肥轻 / 57
71. Lines 131 & 132　策功茂实，勒碑刻铭 / 58
72. Lines 133 & 134　磻溪伊尹，佐时阿衡 / 58
73. Lines 135 & 136　奄宅曲阜，微旦孰营 / 60
74. Lines 137 & 138　桓公匡合，济弱扶倾 / 62
75. Lines 139 & 140　绮回汉惠，说感武丁 / 63
76. Lines 141 & 142　俊乂密勿，多士寔宁 / 65
77. Lines 143 & 144　晋楚更霸，赵魏困横 / 66
78. Lines 145 & 146　假途灭虢，践土会盟 / 68
79. Lines 147 & 148　何遵约法，韩弊烦刑 / 69

80. Lines 149 & 150　起翦颇牧，用军最精 / 72

81. Lines 151 & 152　宣威沙漠，驰誉丹青 / 74

82. Lines 153 & 154　九州禹迹，百郡秦并 / 74

83. Lines 155 & 156　岳宗泰岱，禅主云亭 / 76

84. Lines 157 & 158　雁门紫塞，鸡田赤城 / 78

85. Lines 159 & 160　昆池碣石，巨野洞庭 / 80

86. Lines 161 & 162　旷远绵邈，岩岫杳冥 / 82

87. Lines 163 & 164　治本于农，务兹稼穑 / 83

88. Lines 165 & 166　俶载南亩，我艺黍稷 / 83

89. Lines 167 & 168　税熟贡新，劝赏黜陟 / 84

90. Lines 169 & 170　孟轲敦素，史鱼秉直 / 84

91. Lines 171 & 172　庶几中庸，劳谦谨敕 / 85

92. Lines 173 & 174　聆音察理，鉴貌辨色 / 86

93. Lines 175 & 176　贻厥嘉猷，勉其祗植 / 87

94. Lines 177 & 178　省躬讥诫，宠增抗极 / 87

95. Lines 179 & 180　殆辱近耻，林皋幸即 / 88

96. Lines 181 & 182　两疏见机，解组谁逼 / 88

97. Lines 183 & 184　索居闲处，沉默寂寥 / 89

98. Lines 185 & 186　求古寻论，散虑逍遥 / 90

99. Lines 187 & 188　欣奏累遣，戚谢欢招 / 90

100. Lines 189 & 190　渠荷的历，园莽抽条 / 91

101. Lines 191 & 192　枇杷晚翠，梧桐蚤凋 / 91

5

102. Lines 193 & 194　陈根委翳，落叶飘摇 / 92
103. Lines 195 & 196　游鹍独运，凌摩绛霄 / 92
104. Lines 197 & 198　耽读玩市，寓目囊箱 / 93
105. Lines 199 & 200　易輶攸畏，属耳垣墙 / 93
106. Lines 201 & 202　具膳餐饭，适口充肠 / 94
107. Lines 203 & 204　饱饫烹宰，饥厌糟糠 / 94
108. Lines 205 & 206　亲戚故旧，老少异粮 / 95
109. Lines 207 & 208　妾御绩纺，侍巾帷房 / 95
110. Lines 209 & 210　纨扇圆絜，银烛炜煌 / 96
111. Lines 211 & 212　昼眠夕寐，蓝笋象床 / 96
112. Lines 213 & 214　弦歌酒宴，接杯举觞 / 97
113. Lines 215 & 216　矫手顿足，悦豫且康 / 97
114. Lines 217 & 218　嫡后嗣续，祭祀蒸尝 / 98
115. Lines 219 & 220　稽颡再拜，悚惧恐惶 / 98
116. Lines 221 & 222　笺牒简要，顾答审详 / 99
117. Lines 223 & 224　骸垢想浴，执热愿凉 / 100
118. Lines 225 & 226　驴骡犊特，骇跃超骧 / 100
119. Lines 227 & 228　诛斩贼盗，捕获叛亡 / 101
120. Lines 229 & 230　布射僚丸，嵇琴阮啸 / 101
121. Lines 231 & 232　恬笔伦纸，钧巧任钓 / 102
122. Lines 233 & 234　释纷利俗，并皆佳妙 / 103
123. Lines 235 & 236　毛施淑姿，工颦妍笑 / 104

124. Lines 237 & 238　年矢每催，曦晖朗曜 / 104

125. Lines 239 & 240　璇玑悬斡，晦魄环照 / 105

126. Lines 241 & 242　指薪修祜，永绥吉劭 / 105

127. Lines 243 & 244　矩步引领，俯仰廊庙 / 106

128. Lines 245 & 246　束带矜庄，徘徊瞻眺 / 107

129. Lines 247 & 248　孤陋寡闻，愚蒙等诮 / 107

130. Lines 249 & 250　谓语助者，焉哉乎也 / 108

The Verse of One Thousand Characters（without annotations）[《千字文》（无注释）] / 109

The *Verse* and Chinese Calligraphy（《千字文》与中国书法）/ 129

Line 1
1. 天地玄黄

【拼音】tiān dì xuán huáng

【英译】The sky is black and the earth is yellow.

【今译】苍天是黑色的,大地是黄色的。

【说明】The source of these four characters is in the part of "Word Explanation" of the second trigram in *The Book of Changes*. The character "玄,xuan" means a color that is deep blue and is almost black. Before the Big Bang, the sky was all black, just like what it is now in the outer space. The earth is yellow because the earth along the Yellow River Valley was yellow. The valley was where the states or kingdoms in the pre-Qin period, the Dynasties of Xia, Shang and Zhou were all established. The plain around the valley was formed with the yellow soil washed away by the river from the northwest plateau.

"天地玄黄"出自《易经》坤卦的《文言》部分。玄在颜色上指的是深蓝近于黑的颜色。在宇宙大爆炸之前,天是一片黑色,如同现在的外太空一样。地是黄色的,因为黄河流域一带的土壤是黄色的。先秦时期的夏商周各朝都在黄河流域建都立国。黄河流域的平原是大河从西北高原上冲刷下来的黄土形成的。

Line 2
2. 宇宙洪荒

【拼音】yǔ zhòu hóng huāng

【英译】The universe is huge and infinite.

【今译】茫茫宇宙辽阔无边。

【说明】The English word "universe" can be expressed by the character "宇". *Huai Nan Zi*, a collection of writings in the West Han period, says that the universe is composed of four sides: the upper, the lower, the right and the left. The character "宙, zhou" means time, the time till now and to the future. "洪荒, hong huang" is the state of the earth five billion years ago. Literally, "洪, hong" means flood. There were very serious floods in the early stages of the earth. "荒, huang" means desolation.

西汉时期有一本文集叫《淮南子》，它说上下左右四方为宇，古往今来的时间叫宙。"洪荒"指地球五十亿年前发大水的样子。从字面上讲,"洪"就是水灾的意思。地球的初始阶段发过很大的洪水。"荒"就是荒芜的意思。

Line 3
3. 日月盈昃

【拼音】rì yuè yíng zè

【英译】The waxing and waning of the sun and the moon.

【今译】太阳有正有斜,月亮有缺有圆。

【说明】Actually, "盈, ying" talks about the fullness of the moon and "昃, ze" the setting of the sun. The earliest calendar that was used in China was based on the observations of the moon, so it is called a lunar calendar. The calendar most people use now is a solar calendar. Many traditional festivals are on lunar calendar days.

事实上,满月叫盈,日落叫昃。中国最早的日历是建立在对月亮的观察的基础上的,所以叫阴历。现在多数人使用阳历。中国的很多节日是按阴历说的。

Line 4
4. 辰宿列张

【拼音】chén xiù liè zhāng

【英译】Stars are placed in the limitless sky.

【今译】星辰布满在无边的天空中。

【说明】These four characters are adopted from *Huai Nan Zi*, in which it says "the sky sets up a sun and a moon and listed groups of stars…" The character "辰, chen" in its broad sense is a holistic name of all stars, and in its narrower sense, it means the Polaris. The character "宿, xiu" means a group of stars. The character can also be pronounced as "su", which means something or somebody that has been in existence for some time; it could also mean "overnight". In Chinese astronomy, the stars are divided into 28 "xiu"s. If you connect the 7 "xiu"s in the east with a line, it looks like a dragon; the 7 in the west like a tiger, the 7 in the south like a rosefinch and the 7 in the north look like two things: a snake and a turtle. Yet, in western countries, the word "constellation" is used, and its equivalent is "座，zuo"。

这四个字引自《淮南子》："天设日月，列星辰……"辰字广义上指所有的星辰；狭义上指的是北辰，亦即北极星。宿字是一组星星的意思。宿也可以念成"sù"，其含义指过去的人和事，也可作过夜解。在中国的天文学里，星星被分成二十八宿。如果你将东面的七宿用一条线连起来，它看上去像一条龙；西面的七宿像虎；南面的七宿像朱雀；北面的七宿像玄武，指由蛇和乌龟组成的灵兽，又名龟蛇。西方天文学里使用"constellation"这个词，它在汉语里的意思就是"座"。

Line 5
5. 寒来暑往

【拼音】hán lái shǔ wǎng

【英译】Winter comes and summer goes.

【今译】冬天来了，夏天又去了。

【说明】These four characters are adopted from *The Book of Changes*, in which it says: when winter comes summer is gone; when summer comes winter is gone. Such mutual replacement constitutes a year.

这四个字引自《易经》:"寒往则暑来,暑往则寒来,寒暑相推,而岁成焉。"

Line 6
6. 秋收冬藏

【拼音】qiū shōu dōng cáng

【英译】To harvest in autumn and to store up in winter.

【今译】秋季里忙着收割,冬天里忙着储藏。

【说明】These four characters are also quoted from *Huai Nan Zi* and are proceeded with another four characters:春生夏长,which means coming to life in spring and growing in summer.

这四个字也出自《淮南子》,不过前面还有四个字:春生夏长。

Line 7
7. 闰余成岁

【拼音】rùn yú chéng suì

【英译】The epact has been accumulated into a month and is inserted into a leap year.

【今译】积累数年的闰余并成一个月，放在闰年里。

【说明】These four characters are quoted from *The Decrees of Yao*, *the Documentation of History*, in which it says, "a year would be complete to use intercalary month to decide the four seasons". In the lunar calendar there are 354 days in a year, and there is a lack of 11 days from the solar calendar, in which there are 365 days in a year. These 11 days are what people call "intercalary days". Such intercalary days in three years add up to 33 days. And every three years, there would be such an added month to make a leap month. But a month can only take 30 days, there are still three days more. Well, if you have 7 leap years in a matter of 19 years, nothing would be left.

这四个字出自《尚书·尧典》："以闰月定四时成岁。"按阴历，一年有354天，比阳历的365天少11天。这11天叫闰余，三年的闰余加起来就是33天。这样，每三年就会多出来一个月，就叫闰月。但是，每个月只有30天，还多出3天来。因此，如果19年闰7次就合适了。

Line 8
8. 律吕调阳

【拼音】lǜ lǚ tiáo yáng

【英译】Ancient people used bamboo pipes to do the tuning and to decide on the weather marking days.

【今译】古人用竹管来调音，并标定不同的节气。

【说明】People used to insert 12 bamboo pipes into the earth. The pipes were placed from the short ones to the longer ones, the ones in the odd number were named "lǜ", which belongs to the "masculine" group; and those in the even number were called "lǚ", which belongs to the "feminine" group. What people did was to insert these pipes in the earth on the shady side of a mountain. The longest was 11.8 inches and the shortest was 6.0 inches. The top of the pipes was on the same level. What happened was, for instance, the longest would produce some notes on the day of Winter Solstice, the sound of which was to set the tune of what is today's "C key"; and the other pipes produced other notes on different days. The "lǜ" and "lǚ" were not only used to set tunes, but also used to mark different weather days.

古时候人们将12根竹管由低到高埋在土里，单数的管叫"律"，双数的管叫"吕"。这些竹管被埋在山阴之处。最长的9寸，最短的4.6寸。管口的上面一边齐。到了冬至那天，最长的管会发出声音，这个声音用来定调，相当于现在的C调；其他的管子会在其他的日子发声。律吕不只是用来调音，还可用来标定不同的节气。

Lines 9 & 10
9. 云腾致雨，露结为霜

【拼音】yún téng zhì yǔ, lù jié wéi shuāng

【英译】The ascending clouds would become rain when contacting cold current; in cold night dew would be condensed into frost.

【今译】云气升到天空，遇冷就形成雨；露水碰上寒夜会凝结为霜。

【说明】Chinese people believe that when the earth substance ascends it would become clouds; when the aerial substance in the sky descends it would become rain.

中国人认为地气上升为云，天气下降为雨。

Lines 11 & 12
10. 金生丽水，玉出昆冈

【拼音】jīn shēng lì shuǐ, yù chū kūn gāng

【英译】Gold is produced in the Lijiang River; jade can be found in the Kunlun mountain.

【今译】金子生于丽江，玉石出自昆仑山岗。

【说明】Lijiang River is also called "Jinsha River", which means golden sand river. In ancient China, jade wares were a symbol of loftiness; it was a habit for gentlemen and scholars to wear a piece of jade.

丽江也叫金沙江。在古代中国，玉象征着高贵。所以，君子都佩玉。

Lines 13 & 14

11. 剑号巨阙，珠称夜光

【拼音】jiàn hào jù què, zhū chēng yè guāng

【英译】The most famous sword is Ju Que; the most precious pearl is called Ye Guang.

【今译】最有名的宝剑叫"巨阙"，最贵重的明珠叫"夜光"。

【说明】In the Spring and Autumn period, the King of the State of Yue—Yun Chang（允常）asked Ouye Zi（欧冶子）to cast five swords. The first one turned out to be the best and it was Ju Que, and the other four were all very famous. Three of them were longer ones and the remaining two were shorter ones. One of the shorter was called Yu Chang, which means "fish intestine". It was used by Zhuan Zhu（专诸）to kill King Liao of Wu（吴王僚）. Zhuan succeeded by hiding the dagger in the fish. From that time on, if you say "three things longer and two shorter" is happening to somebody, you mean an unexpected disaster is falling onto this person.

春秋时期，越王允常请欧冶子为他铸造五把剑。第一把剑是最好的，叫巨阙，其他四把也很有名。这五把剑三长两短。有一把短剑叫鱼肠，是专诸用来刺杀吴王僚的。专诸将短剑藏在鱼腹内，所以能刺杀成功。从那时起，"三长两短"就用来形容意外的灾祸了。

Line 14 is quoted from the story of *Searching for the Deity*（《搜神记》）. The story says one Marquis from the State of Sui saved the life of a snake, who came back to thank the Marquis and gave him a big pearl, which shone in the night, and was called Ye Guang.

第14句是一个引自《搜神记》的故事，说隋国的一位诸侯救了一条蛇，这条蛇后来找到他，送给他一颗珍珠，此珠夜里发光，叫夜明珠。

Lines 15 & 16
12. 果珍李柰，菜重芥姜

【拼音】guǒ zhēn lǐ nài, cài zhòng jiè jiāng

【英译】The best fruits are plum and apple; the most important vegetables are leaf mustard and ginger.

【今译】果子中最珍贵的是李和柰，蔬菜中最重要的是芥和姜。

【说明】"柰" has a Latin name: rhizoma kaempferiae. It is

something like an apple.

柰的拉丁文名称是"rhizoma kaempferiae",它是一种像苹果的水果。

Lines 17 & 18
13. 海咸河淡，鳞潜羽翔

【拼音】hǎi xián hé dàn, lín qián yǔ xiáng

【英译】Sea water is salty and river water is fresh; fish swims in the water and birds fly in the sky.

【今译】海水咸，河水淡，鱼儿在水中潜游，鸟儿在空中飞翔。

Lines 19 & 20
14. 龙师火帝，鸟官人皇

【拼音】lóng shī huǒ dì, niǎo guān rén huáng

【英译】The Dragon Teacher, the Fire Emperor, the Bird Officer and the Human Emperor were all emperors in the ancient times.

【今译】龙师和火帝、鸟官和人皇都是上古时代的帝皇。

【说明】According to legends, Fu Xi（伏羲）used to use the word "dragon" to name his officials, and he was thus called the "Dragon Teacher". He was the one who found the "Eight Trigrams" and discovered fishing. He was in power for 115 years. Shen Nong（神农）used "fire" to name his officials and he was thus called the "Fire Emperor". He was the one who taught people how to farm and discovered herbal medicine. He was in power for 140 years.

根据传说，伏羲用"龙"来称呼他的手下，所以，他也被称为"龙师"。伏羲发现了"八卦"，发明了捕鱼，当政115年。神农用"火"来称呼他的手下，所以他又被称为"火帝"。他教人民如何耕种，还发现了草药，当政140年。

Shao Hao（少昊），son of the Yellow Emperor, was called "Bird Officer" because he named his officials with birds. The Human Emperor was one of the three legendary emperors. According to *Records of the Historian*, he had nine heads, drove a cart in the clouds with six big birds. His ruled for 150 generations, which added up to 45,600 years.

少昊是黄帝的儿子，人们称他为"鸟官"，因为他用鸟来称呼他的手下。人皇是三皇之一。据《史记》记载，人皇长有9个头，用6只大鸟云中驾车。他的统治传了150代，共45 600年。

Lines 21 & 22
15. 始制文字，乃服衣裳

【拼音】shǐ zhì wén zì, nǎi fú yī cháng

【英译】Characters were invented; people began to put on cloths.

【今译】汉字被创造出来，人们开始穿衣遮体。

【说明】People believe it was Cang Jie（仓颉）who invented the characters. He was an official responsible for noting down important events for historic records during the reign of Huang Di（黄帝 or the Yellow Emperor）. It is said that after he invented the characters, it rained and ghosts cried at night.

人们认为仓颉发明了汉字。他本是黄帝记录事件的史官。据说，他发明汉字后，天上下了雨，鬼神在夜里哭泣。

It was Lei Zu（嫘祖）who made the first set of clothing. She was the wife of Huang Di and the first person to breed silkworms, and was therefore able to make clothing.

是嫘祖制作了人类第一套衣服。她是黄帝的妻子,是第一个养蚕人,所以能够做衣服。

Lines 23 & 24
16. 推位让国,有虞陶唐

【拼音】tuī wèi ràng guó, yǒu yú táo táng

【英译】To give the throne and state power to those who were meritorious, capable and wise. That happened in the tribes of Youyu and Taotang.

【今译】(唐尧和虞舜)把君位禅让给功臣贤人。禅让的事发生在有虞和陶唐两个部落。

【说明】Both Yao (尧) and Shun (舜) passed throne and state power to others who were not their family members. Yao was the head of a tribe for 70 years. Yao chose Shun to succeed him. We don't have Shun's dates of birth and death.

尧和舜都将皇帝宝座和国家权力传给了家族以外的人。尧是部落首领,在位 70 年。尧选了舜来继任。舜的生卒年不详。

Youyu (有虞) was the tribe of which Shun was its chief. Taotang (陶唐) was the tribe of Yao. Shun ruled for 50 years and then he passed on the power to Yu（禹）.

有虞是一个部落，舜是其首领。陶唐是尧的部落。舜当政 50 年，然后将权力传给了禹。

Lines 25 & 26
17. 吊民伐罪，周发殷汤

【拼音】diào mín fá zuì, zhōu fā yīn tāng

【英译】To pacify people and punish the criminal was what King Wu of Zhou and King Tang of Shang did.

【今译】安抚百姓，讨伐暴君，是周武王姬发和商君成汤做的事情。

【说明】The name of King Wu of Zhou was Ji Fa. He toppled the rule of King Zhou of Shang and founded the Zhou Dynasty. The Shang Dynasty was also called the Yin. It was established by King Tang who defeated Jie, the ruler of the Xia.

周武王叫姬发。他打败了商纣王，建立了周朝。商朝也叫殷朝，由汤王打败夏桀所建。

Lines 27 & 28
18. 坐朝问道，垂拱平章

【拼音】zuò cháo wèn dào, chuí gǒng píng zhāng

【英译】They sat in their throne and discussed state affairs with their officials; since the state was peaceful and achievements were very outstanding, what they did was only hanging up their gowns and folding their hands to show their appreciation.

【今译】他们坐在龙位上，与大臣们共商国是。由于天下太平，事业兴旺，他们不需要做什么事情，只需要垂衣拱手就够了。

【说明】Having adopted good policies and put right persons on right posts, they didn't have to make themselves busy.

在实行了好的政策，将正确的人安放在正确的位置上之后，他们就不必自己忙乎了。

Lines 29 & 30
19. 爱育黎首，臣伏戎羌

【拼音】ài yù lí shǒu, chén fú róng qiāng

【英译】They cared about the common folks; tribes like Rong and Qiang all bowed to them.

【今译】他们爱抚、体恤老百姓，戎和羌这样的部落都归附了他们。

Lines 31 & 32
20. 遐迩一体，率宾归王

【拼音】xiá ěr yī tǐ, shuài bīn guī wáng

【英译】Places far and near had come into one unified country; people in the four seas were all subjects of the King.

【今译】远远近近都统一在一起，四海之内的人民全都心甘情愿地臣服贤君。

Lines 33 & 34
21. 鸣凤在竹，白驹食场

【拼音】míng fèng zài zhú, bái jū shí chǎng

【英译】Phoenixes are chirping happily in the bamboo

forest; white horses are eating grass in the field.

【今译】凤凰在竹林中欢鸣,白马在草场上觅食。

Lines 35 & 36
22. 化被草木,赖及万方

【拼音】huà bèi cǎo mù, lài jí wàn fāng

【英译】Even grass and trees were touched by the rule of virtue; benefits have reached to everyone in every corner of the country.

【今译】贤君的教化覆盖大自然的一草一木,恩泽遍及天下百姓。

小结

The above can be considered as the first part of the *Verse*. It begins with the birth of the universe, and then provides us with a general picture of the ancient history of China.

以上可以看作《千字文》的第一部分。它从宇宙诞生开始,给我们绘制了一幅中国简史的图画。

Lines 37 & 38
23. 盖此身发，四大五常

【拼音】gài cǐ shēn fà, sì dà wǔ cháng

【英译】As far as our flesh and hair are concerned, they resemble four major factors and they should function in five consistencies.

【今译】人的身体发肤分属于"四大"，身发都要按"五常"行事。

【说明】The four major factors are physical: earth, water, fire and wind; the five consistencies are spiritual: kindness, justice, propriety, intelligence and trust.

四大因素就是地水火风，五常就是仁义礼智信。

Lines 39 & 40
24. 恭惟鞠养，岂敢毁伤

【拼音】gōng wéi jū yǎng, qǐ gǎn huǐ shāng

【英译】Caution is needed to take good care of them, people should never venture to harm them.

【今译】承蒙父母生养爱护,身体发肤不可有一丝一毫的毁坏损伤。

【说明】These characters are adopted from *The Classic of Filial Duties*, which is a dialogue between Confucius and his disciple Zengzi(曾子)on the matter of filial duties. It says in the beginning, "the hair and skin of our body are given by our parents; people should never dare to harm them". The body is where conscience and thoughts reside. It is only lent to us by our parents, and it should be returned after usage. If you damaged it or wounded it, how can you return it to your parents? In such a sense, you are expected to foster the body with respect and care.

这几个字出自《孝经》,它记录了孔子与曾子关于孝道的谈话。《孝经》在开头说:"身体发肤,受之父母,不敢毁伤。"我们的身体是神智和思想居住的地方,是父母借给我们的,使用完还要归还。如果你毁伤了它,该如何归还呢?从这个意义上讲,你必须用心照看你的身体。

Lines 41 & 42
25. 女慕贞洁，男效才良

【拼音】nǚ mù zhēn jié, nán xiào cái liáng

【英译】Girls adore integrity and cleanness; boys imitate virtuous and talented persons.

【今译】女子应仰慕那些为人称道的贞洁妇女，男子应仿效那些德才兼备的贤人。

【说明】The character "贞，zhen" is borrowed from *The Book of Changes*. One of the features of the first hexagram "Qian" was "firmness in integrity".

"贞"字出自《易经》的乾卦，是正直坚定的意思。

Lines 43 & 44
26. 知过必改，得能莫忘

【拼音】zhī guò bì gǎi, dé néng mò wàng

【英译】Mistakes must be corrected when you are aware of

them; do not give up when it is within your ability.

【今译】知道自己有过错，一定要改正；有能力办到的事，不要放弃。

【说明】This thought is borrowed from *Analects of Confucius*, in which Confucius says there were four things that worry him constantly, and one of them was that people do not correct their mistakes when they were aware of them.

这个观点借自《论语》。孔子说有四件事情让他忧愁，其中之一就是知错不改。

Lines 45 & 46
27. 罔谈彼短，靡恃己长

【拼音】wǎng tán bǐ duǎn, mǐ shì jǐ cháng

【英译】Don't talk about the shortcomings of others; don't be conceited over one's own strong points.

【今译】不要去谈论别人的短处，也不要依仗自己有长处就自我满足。

Lines 47 & 48
28. 信使可覆，器欲难量

【拼音】xìn shǐ kě fù, qì yù nán liáng

【英译】One's trustworthiness should stand tests; it is difficult to measure one's magnanimities.

【今译】诚实的话要能经受时间的考验，一个人的度量让人难以估量。

Lines 49 & 50
29. 墨悲丝染，诗赞羔羊

【拼音】mò bēi sī rǎn, shī zàn gāo yáng

【英译】Mozi was sad when he saw white silk threads dyed into other colors; *The Book of Songs* sings praises of lamb.

【今译】墨子为白丝染色不褪而悲泣，《诗经》中有赞颂"羔羊"的诗篇。

【说明】This story is adopted from *The Book of Mozi*, in which he says: "It is grey when dyed with the color of grey, and yellow with the color of yellow … One got to be careful." The story may imply that a person's nature is as white and clean as the white silk threads. It would be almost impossible to restore to the original color if it is stained.

这个故事引自《墨子》，其中有这样的话："染于苍则苍，染于黄则黄，……不可不慎也。"这个故事暗喻了人的本性像生丝一样洁白，一旦被染了色，再想恢复本性的质朴纯洁，已经不可能了。

In *The Book of Songs*, there is one poem describing the purity of lamb in the section of ballads.

《诗经》的"风"部，有一篇描写羔羊洁白的诗歌。

Lines 51 & 52
30. 景行维贤，克念作圣

【拼音】jǐng xíng wéi xián, kè niàn zuò shèng

【英译】People admire the virtue and behavior of capable persons; they should also check their desires and follow suit of saints.

【今译】人们羡慕贤人高尚的品德；也要克制私欲，努力仿效圣人。

Lines 53 & 54
31. 德建名立，形端表正

【拼音】dé jiàn míng lì, xíng duān biǎo zhèng

【英译】When virtue is fostered fame would come; only when one carries himself properly his appearance would look respectable.

【今译】养成了好的道德，就会有好的名声；举止端庄，其仪表也会受人尊敬。

Lines 55 & 56
32. 空谷传声，虚堂习听

【拼音】kōng gǔ chuán shēng, xū táng xí tīng

【英译】Sound goes far in an empty valley; voice can be heard very clearly in a spacious hall.

【今译】空旷的山谷中呼喊声传得很远，宽敞的厅堂里说话声非常清晰。

Lines 57 & 58
33. 祸因恶积，福缘善庆

【拼音】huò yīn è jī, fú yuán shàn qìng

【英译】Misfortune is caused by the accumulation of evil; fortune is an outcome of prodigal benefactions.

【今译】祸害是因为多次作恶积累而成，幸福是由于常年行善得到的奖赏。

【说明】These two lines are adopted from *The Book of Changes*, in which it says: A family of good deeds enjoys surplus fortune; trouble awaits a family of bad deeds in the corner.

这两行字引自《易经》，书中说，"积善之家必有余庆，积不善之家必有余殃"。

Lines 59 & 60
34. 尺璧非宝，寸阴是竞

【拼音】chǐ bì fēi bǎo, cùn yīn shì jìng

【英译】A foot long piece of jade should not be regarded as a treasure; a short span of time must be grasped.

【今译】一尺长的璧玉算不上宝贵，一寸短的光阴却值得去争取。

【说明】These two lines are adopted from *Huai Nan Zi*, in which it says: "A saint does not take a foot long piece of jade as precious, yet takes an inch of time as a treasure."

这两句话引自《淮南子》，书中有这样的话："圣人不贵尺之璧，而重寸之阴。"

Lines 61 & 62
35. 资父事君，曰严与敬

【拼音】zī fù shì jūn, yuē yán yǔ jìng

【英译】In looking after the father and providing service to the King, one should take pains and be respectful.

【今译】供养父亲，侍奉国君，要做到认真、谨慎、恭敬。

【说明】Five relationships are being discussed now, which are that between child and father, husband and wife, brothers, friends and that with the king (or monarch). The guiding principles for these relationships are respectively kindness, justice, propriety, intelligence and trust.

从这里开始讨论五伦关系，亦即父子、夫妇、兄弟、朋友和君臣。处理这些关系的指导原则是仁义礼智信。

Lines 63 & 64
36. 孝当竭力，忠则尽命

【拼音】xiào dāng jié lì, zhōng zé jìn mìng

【英译】One should do his best in performing his filial duties; one should pledge loyalty to the monarch.

【今译】对父母孝，要尽心竭力；对国君忠，要竭尽本分。

【说明】Some people interpreted line 64 as "one should even give his life in the loyalty to the monarch". The character "命, ming" can mean "life", but here it can also mean "exerting one's due". If "命, ming" only means "life", it is not proper for the author to use "尽, jin" before "命, ming", for a person has only one life, you give your life or you don't. The word "尽, jin" means to do your best, or to exert your efforts; so, to exert one's life, does not mean giving one's life. Both Confucius and Mencius were against blind loyalty. Mencius even said that if the monarch is a despot, people should overthrow him.

有人将第 64 句译为：忠于君主不惜生命。"命"可以解释为生命，但是，它也有"尽本分"的意思。如果"命"只作生命讲，那么，人只有一次生命，要么你献出生命，要么你保留生命。但是"尽"是尽力而为的意思。所以，"尽命"不是牺牲性命的意思。不管是孔子，还是孟子，都反对愚忠。孟子甚至讲，如果君王是个暴君，人民就应推翻他的统治。

Lines 65 & 66
37. 临深履薄，夙兴温凊

【拼音】lín shēn lǚ bó，sù xīng wēn qìng

【英译】Be most careful as if one is on the verge of an abyss or on top of a thin layer of ice. To rise up early and sit up late in order to make sure your parents are warm in winter and cool in summer.

【今译】要"如临深渊，如履薄冰"那样小心谨慎；要早起晚睡，让父母冬暖夏凉。

【说明】Line 65 is adopted from *The Book of Songs*. One poem in the part of "Minor Grace" says: to be trembling as if they were on the verge of an abyss or on top of a thin layer of ice. These four characters suggest a kind of attitude in rendering service to the king or monarch.

"临深履薄"引自《诗经》。"小雅"中有篇诗歌说:"战战兢兢,如临深渊,如履薄冰。"这几个字说明了为君王服务时应有的态度。

Line 66 is a short form for "夙兴夜寐" and "冬温夏凊", which means "to rise up early and sit up late" and the parents are "warm in winter and cool in summer". In ancient times these were what requested of children of a family, that is to say, children were supposed to get up earlier and go to bed later than their parents, of which the purpose was to make sure parents were physically alright at these hours.

"夙兴温凊"是"夙兴夜寐"和"冬温夏凊"两个成语的缩写。其含义是:早起晚睡,冬天(让父母)温暖,夏天(让父母)清凉。在中国古代,子女要做到这两点,也就是说,子女要比父母起得早,睡得晚,之所以如此,是因为子女要确保父母在早晚身体都无恙。

Lines 67 & 68
38. 似兰斯馨,如松之盛

【拼音】sì lán sī xīn, rú sōng zhī shèng

32

【英译】One's virtue should be as fragrant as orchid, and as flourishing as pine.

【今译】能做到上面所说的那样,德行就同兰花一样馨香,同青松一样茂盛。

Lines 69 & 70
39. 川流不息,渊澄取映

【拼音】chuān liú bù xī, yuān chéng qǔ yìng

【英译】Our virtue should reach our posterity like the forever running water in the river; the virtue of our progenitor is so clear and reflective like the water in an abyss.

【今译】德行要能延及子孙,像大河一样川流不息;祖先的品德影响世人,就像碧潭清澄照人。

Lines 71 & 72
40. 容止若思,言辞安定

【拼音】róng zhǐ ruò sī, yán cí ān dìng

【英译】You should carry yourself in a serene and

composed way and give an impression that you are deep in thought; your words should sound definite and pacifying.

【今译】仪态举止要庄重，看上去若有所思；语气要肯定，显得从容沉静。

【说明】The above two lines are adopted from "The Amenity for Trifling Matters", which is a part of *The Book of Rites*, which says: Never be impudent, you should look serious in thought and your words should be certain and convincing.

上面的两句话引自《礼记·曲礼》，此书中说，"毋不敬，俨若思，安定辞"。

Lines 73 & 74
41. 笃初诚美，慎终宜令

【拼音】dǔ chū chéng měi, shèn zhōng yí lìng

【英译】A solid beginning is of course beautiful, yet, it is better to have a good ending.

【今译】有好的开头固然不错，有好的结果更为重要。

Lines 75 & 76
42. 荣业所基，籍甚无竟

【拼音】róng yè suǒ jī, jí shèn wú jìng

【英译】Such is the basis for fame and achievement; having had such a foundation, the prospect of one's fame and profession would be limitless.

【今译】这些就是荣誉和成就的根基，有这样的根基，就会有无尽的显耀和事业的成功。

【说明】The basis would include a solid beginning, a good ending and the performer's virtue.

这个基础包括一个牢靠的开端、一个好的结尾和创业人的品德。

Lines 77 & 78
43. 学优登仕，摄职从政

【拼音】xué yōu dēng shì, shè zhí cóng zhèng

【英译】Those whose studies are the best could be officials;

an official would then perform duties and handle political matters.

【今译】学习出色并有余力，就可走上仕道（做官）；担任一定的职务，就可以参与国家的政事。

【说明】Line 77 is quoted from the 13th paragraph of the 19th chapter of *Analects of Confucius*. This paragraph is a saying of Zi Xia（子夏）：He who has more efforts in being an official should study; he who has more efforts in studying can become an official. But it has been very common for most people to remember the latter part as：to be an official you got to be the best in studies. Zhu Xi（朱熹）, an influential Confucian scholar in the Song Dynasty interpreted the sentence as：the studies on an official post would support his career in a profound way; to be an official after one has studied would testify broadly what he has learned.

"学优登仕"引自《论语》第19章第13段，这是子夏说的一句话："仕而优则学，学而优则仕。"但是，大多数人都记住了后面一句话。宋朝的大儒朱熹这样解释这两句话："仕而学则所以资其仕者益深，学而仕则所以验其学者益广。"

Lines 79 & 80
44. 存以甘棠，去而益咏

【拼音】cún yǐ gān táng, qù ér yì yǒng

【英译】Efforts have been made to keep alive the birchleaf pear. The longer Count Shao of the Zhou Dynasty has died, the more people would sing praises of him.

【今译】人们千方百计地保护甘棠树，召公过世越久老百姓越怀念并歌咏他。

【说明】Why did people do so? Because it was under this tree, Ji Shi（姬奭）, a Count of the Zhou Dynasty, handled legal and political matters to the satisfaction of everybody, including the nobilities and the common folks. People used to address him as Count Shao of the Zhou Dynasty（周召公）. Taking good care of the tree had become a way for the local people to remember him. It has been found where this tree was. There are some records in the genealogy of the Zhou Family at Yongming County of Hunan Province.

人们为什么这么做呢？因为周召公姬奭曾在这棵树下处理政务。他为官不但贵族满意，老百姓也满意。人们都称他为周召公。千方百计养活这棵树，是人们纪念他的一种方式。现在，已经找到了这棵树所在的地方。湖南"永明周氏族谱"中对此事有专门的记载。

Line 81
45. 乐殊贵贱

【拼音】yuè shū guì jiàn

【英译】Music may vary according to the status of people, noble or humble.

【今译】选择乐曲要根据人的身份贵贱有所不同。

【说明】Music played an important role in the life of ancient Chinese. The culture in the pre-Qin period can be termed as "propriety and music". Music was one of the skills every school attendant must acquire. There were plucking percussion and wind instruments. Music was very closely linked with rites and protocol.

在古代中国人的生活里，音乐起着重要的作用。先秦的文化可以叫作"礼乐文化"。音乐是每个上学的孩子都要学的。那时已有弹拨乐器、打击乐器和吹奏乐器。音乐与仪礼关系密切。

Line 82
46. 礼别尊卑

【拼音】lǐ bié zūn bēi

【英译】Propriety to the lowly is different from that to the lofty.

【今译】采用礼节要按照人的地位高低有所区别。

【说明】Rites and protocol was a way of life before the Spring and Autumn period. Confucius tried his best to resume the social order of propriety and music in his life time. There are three books in the Confucian classics talking about rites, etiquette and formalities. The ultimate aim of practicing rites was to find harmony or striking a balance in the society.

春秋之前,仪礼是一种生活方式。孔子活着的时候,力图恢复礼乐的社会秩序。在儒学的经典里有三本关于礼仪的书籍。实行礼制的最终目的是使社会和谐或者使社会平衡发展。

Lines 83 & 84
47. 上和下睦，夫唱妇随

【拼音】shàng hé xià mù, fū chàng fù suí

【英译】There should be harmony between the older and the younger; one would follow what his/her spouse has proposed.

【今译】长辈和小辈要和睦相处，夫妇要一唱一随，协调和谐。

Lines 85 & 86
48. 外受傅训，入奉母仪

【拼音】wài shòu fù xùn, rù fèng mǔ yí

【英译】One should accept the instruction of teachers outside; one should follow the norms of mother at home.

【今译】在外面要听从师长的教诲，在家里要遵守母亲的规范。

【说明】The Chinese society attaches much importance to

teachers. It was believed that a teacher for one day should be respected as a father all his life. A teacher was often held liable for the blunder of his student. A teacher should not only pass on knowledge to his students, but also teach them how to be a good person and how to behave in the society. Education of children used to be the duty of the mother in the family, because the father was often not home in a year. So the typical duty of a wife was to support her husband and to educate her children.

中国社会尊师重教,有"一日为师,终身为父"的说法。学生有过失,老师是要负责任的。老师不但要传授知识,还要教学生如何做人,如何在社会中表现。在家中往往是母亲负责对孩子的教育,因为父亲常年不在家。所以,一个妻子的职责是相夫教子。

Lines 87 & 88
49. 诸姑伯叔,犹子比儿

【拼音】zhū gū bó shū, yóu zǐ bǐ ér

【英译】Treat your aunts and uncles like your parents; aunts and uncles should treat their nephews like their own children.

【今译】对待姑姑、伯伯、叔叔等长辈要像对待亲生父母一样，叔伯对待侄子、侄女要像对他们的亲生子女一样。

【说明】In Confucian thoughts there are three things to do to be kindly sympathetic: the first thing is to be dear to your relatives; the second thing is to care about others; and the third thing is to love the nature and things in it.

在儒家的思想里，要为仁必须做三件事情：第一，对家人亲戚要好；第二，要关心他人；第三，热爱自然和自然中的事物。

Lines 89 & 90
50. 孔怀兄弟，同气连枝

【拼音】kǒng huái xiōng dì, tóng qì lián zhī

【英译】One should be most concerned with his brothers; because they inherit the same blood and vital energy from their parents, they are like branches on the same tree that have the same roots.

【今译】兄弟之间要非常相爱，因为同受父母血气，犹如树枝相连。

【说明】Line 89 is adopted from a poem in *The Book of*

Songs. The relation among brothers is one of the five relationships. What has been stressed is that the younger should respect the older. If the father has passed away, the oldest brother would become the master of the family.

第89句出自《诗经》。兄弟之间的关系是五伦之一。这里强调的是弟弟要尊敬兄长。如果家中父亲去世了，就由长子当家。

Lines 91 & 92
51. 交友投分，切磨箴规

【拼音】jiāo yǒu tóu fèn, qiē mó zhēn guī

【英译】The friends you make should be congenial to you, and be able to discuss studies with you and give you admonition.

【今译】结交朋友要意气相投，学习上切磋琢磨，品行上互相告勉。

Lines 93 & 94
52. 仁慈隐恻，造次弗离

【拼音】rén cí yǐn cè, zào cì fú lí

【英译】A feeling of commiseration contains kindness and affection; in urgency such a feeling should never be given up.

【今译】仁义、慈爱，以及对人的恻隐之心，在最仓促、危急的情况下也不能抛离。

【说明】In Confucian thoughts human beings have a good nature.

在儒家的思想里，人性本善。

Lines 95 & 96
53. 节义廉退，颠沛匪亏

【拼音】jié yì lián tuì, diān pèi fěi kuī

【英译】Integrity, justice, cleanness and modesty are indispensible, even at times of adversity.

【今译】正直、正义、廉洁、谦让的美德，在最穷困潦倒的时候也不可亏缺。

【说明】Integrity to some extent is trust. Justice is the highest principle, for which one can give his life. To be clean on the official post needs intelligence. To be modest is to show respect to others. So these are the five consistencies if you add kindness.

正直在一定程度上讲就是信誉。义是最高的原则，可以舍生取义。在官位上保持廉洁需要智慧。谦让是对别人的尊敬。如果再加上仁，五常就全了。

Lines 97 & 98
54. 性静情逸，心动神疲

【拼音】xìng jìng qíng yì, xīn dòng shén pí

【英译】A calm heart brings ease and comfort; a restless heart would make you exhausted.

【今译】品性沉静淡泊，情绪就安逸自在；内心浮躁好动，精神就疲惫困倦。

Lines 99 & 100
55. 守真志满，逐物意移

【拼音】shǒu zhēn zhì mǎn, zhú wù yì yí

【英译】A pure heart would fulfill your aspirations; your will would be altered if you chase after material needs.

【今译】保持纯洁的天性，就会实现抱负；追求物欲享受，意志就会被改变。

Lines 101 & 102
56. 坚持雅操，好爵自縻

【拼音】jiān chí yǎ cāo, hǎo jué zì mí

【英译】To persist in elegant integrity, you would be automatically tied to a good luck.

【今译】坚持高尚的情操，好的运气自然会找到你。

小结

This is the end of the second part, which tells us the relationship between virtue and fame, body and heart. It shows us how to behave well and keep our pure heart.

第二部分在这里结束。此部分告诉我们道德和声誉、身体和思想的关系。它告诉我们应如何端正行为，如何保持内心的纯洁。

Lines 103 & 104
57. 都邑华夏，东西二京

【拼音】dū yì huá xià, dōng xī èr jīng

【英译】The capital cities of ancient China are magnificent; there was one capital in the east and one capital in the west in different periods.

【今译】古代的都城华美壮观，有东西二京洛阳和长安。

【说明】Luoyang（洛阳）was the capital city for many dynasties. Chang'an（长安）which is today's Xi'an（西安）was also the capital city for many dynasties or regimes.

洛阳是多个朝代的都城。长安亦即今日之西安，也是多个朝代或政权的都城。

Lines 105 & 106
58. 背邙面洛，浮渭据泾

【拼音】bèi máng miàn luò, fú wèi jù jīng

【英译】Luoyang has Mount Mang at its back and Luo River at its front; River Wei is on the left side of Xi'an and River Jing is on its right side.

【今译】东京洛阳背靠北邙山（亦称"邙山"），南临洛水；西京长安左跨渭河，右依泾水。

【说明】Owing to its mild climate and quality of soil, many royal cemeteries were built there. People used to think that an ideal life was to be born in Suzhou or Hangzhou and to be buried after death at Mount Mang.

由于气候宜人,土壤肥厚,许多皇室的陵园就设在邙山。历史上素有"生于苏杭,葬于北邙"之说。

Lines 107 & 108
59. 宫殿盘郁,楼观飞惊

【拼音】gōng diàn pán yù, lóu guàn fēi jīng

【英译】Many palaces and halls seem to overlap each other on the winding roads; people are startled at the sight of the seemingly flying towers.

【今译】宫殿错综曲折,重重叠叠;楼阁高耸入云,令人震惊。

【说明】A palace is a place for living of the royal family; a hall is normally an office for the emperors or kings to work in.

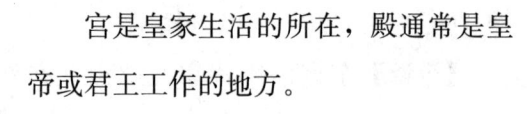

宫是皇家生活的所在,殿通常是皇帝或君王工作的地方。

Lines 109 & 110
60. 图写禽兽，画彩仙灵

【拼音】tú xiě qín shòu, huà cǎi xiān líng

【英译】Birds and animals are painted on the walls of the palaces and halls; there are also immortals and deities painted in colors.

【今译】宫殿上绘着各种飞禽走兽，描画出五彩的天仙神灵。

Lines 111 & 112
61. 丙舍傍启，甲帐对楹

【拼音】bǐng shè páng qǐ, jiǎ zhàng duì yíng

【英译】The doors of auxiliary halls are also on the side; opposite to the front columns are draperies decorated with pearls, coral and precious jade.

【今译】正殿两边的配殿在侧面开门，用珍珠、玛瑙和玉石装饰的帐幕对着高高的楹柱。

49

Lines 113 & 114
62. 肆筵设席，鼓瑟吹笙

【拼音】sì yán shè xí, gǔ sè chuī shēng

【英译】Tables and seats are prepared for banquets; string and pipe instruments are played.

【今译】宫殿中大摆宴席，乐师鼓瑟吹笙。

【说明】"瑟, se" is a 25-string plucking instrument. "笙, sheng" is a bamboo wind instrument.

瑟是有25根弦的弹拨乐器，笙是竹子做的吹奏乐器。

Lines 115 & 116
63. 升阶纳陛，弁转疑星

【拼音】shēng jiē nà bì, biàn zhuǎn yí xīng

【英译】The officials are climbing up the steps; the jade inlaid on the caps of officials is glittering like stars.

【今译】文武百官登上台阶进入殿堂，他们镶在帽子上的美玉，像满天的星星。

【说明】Steps in ordinary buildings are called "阶, jie"; steps in the imperial court are called "陛, bi". When officials report to the emperor under the steps, they often call themselves "Bi Xia", which means: I who stand under the steps. "弁, bian" is an official cap. There were black caps and leather caps. Leather caps were often inlaid with jade pieces.

一般建筑物的台阶叫"阶",皇宫里的台阶叫"陛"。臣子站在陛阶之下向天子奏事,自称陛下。意为"在陛下者告之",就是站在台阶底下的我有事要奏报。"弁"就是官帽,有爵弁和皮弁之分。皮弁上经常镶嵌有宝石。

Lines 117 & 118
64. 右通广内,左达承明

【拼音】yòu tōng guǎng nèi, zuǒ dá chéng míng

【英译】To the right of the main hall is the Guang Nei Hall, the Imperial Library; the Cheng Ming Hall is on the left.

【今译】建章宫右面通向用以藏书的广内殿,左面通向朝臣休息的承明殿。

【说明】This is talking about the western capital Chang'an. To the right from the main hall—the Jian Zhang Hall, is the Guang Nei Hall. The Cheng Ming Hall was where officials used to have a rest.

这说的是西京长安。主殿叫建章宫，它的右边是广内殿。承明殿是朝臣休息的地方。

Lines 119 & 120
65. 既集坟典，亦聚群英

【拼音】jì jí fén diǎn, yì jù qún yīng

【英译】These are places where classic works are collected, and places that gather heroes and talents.

【今译】这里收藏了很多的典籍名著，也聚集着成群的文武英才。

【说明】"坟典，fen dian" are respectively books about the earliest three leaders and books about the five emperors.

关于三皇的书叫"坟"，关于五帝的书叫"典"。

Lines 121 & 122
66. 杜稿钟隶，漆书壁经

【拼音】dù gǎo zhōng lì, qī shū bì jīng

【英译】There you can find Du Du's manuscript and Zhong Yao's calligraphy, and characters written with resin, and classics hidden in walls are also available.

【今译】宫殿中有杜度的草书、钟繇的隶书，还有用漆写的古籍和孔壁中的经典。

【说明】Du Du（杜度）was a famous calligrapher in the Eastern Han period, and he was the first one who wrote in the cursive script. Zhong Yao（钟繇，151-230）was an important calligrapher in the Three Kingdoms period, and his clerical script was influential. Before ink was discovered, Chinese people used resin to write on bamboo slips. Some books were discovered from inside the screen wall in the courtyard of the residence of Confucius after the reign of Qin came to an end. These books are *The Classic of Filial Duties*, *Documentation of History* and *Analects of Confucius*. They were inside the wall because people feared that they might be burnt by the rulers of Qin, as it happened in other places in that period.

杜度是东汉著名的书法家,他是第一个写草书的人。钟繇(151—230)是三国时期重要的书法家,其隶书对后人的影响很大。在墨被发现之前,人们用漆在竹子上写字。秦朝灭亡后,人们在孔府影壁的夹缝里找到了《孝经》、《尚书》和《论语》。这些书之所以藏在影壁里,是害怕被秦朝的统治者烧掉。秦"焚书"时烧掉了不少书。

Lines 123 & 124
67. 府罗将相,路侠槐卿

【拼音】fǔ luó jiàng xiàng, lù jiā① huái qīng

【英译】Civil and military officials were gathered in the hall; dukes and highest officials stood along the road outside the hall in the palace.

【今译】宫廷内将相依次排成两列,宫廷外大夫公卿夹道站立。

---

① 侠:今读"xiá",此处通"夹"。

【说明】"槐，huai" is the Chinese scholar tree, and is used to represent the three dukes (Grand Tutor, Grand Teacher and Grand Guardian); "卿，qing" refers to the highest officials in the royal court and the administration.

"槐"在中文里指中国学者之树，它通常用来代指三公（如太师、太傅和太保等）；"卿"指皇宫和内阁里级别最高的官员。

Lines 125 & 126
68. 户封八县，家给千兵

【拼音】hù fēng bā xiàn, jiā jǐ qiān bīng

【英译】The fief granted to every highest official is as big as eight counties; each family was provided with a team of guards of over one thousand men.

【今译】高官们每户有八县之广的封地，并配备上千的士兵。

【说明】Eight counties here only indicate the size of the fief was big, and it should not be read as a specific figure, because in history nobody has ever been given a fief of the size of eight counties. Again, the word thousand should not be read as an accurate figure.

八县泛指封地之大，此处不要当成具体的数字。因为在历史上从未有人的封地有八县之大。同样地，此处的千也不要当成准确的数字。

Lines 127 & 128
69. 高冠陪辇，驱毂振缨

【拼音】gāo guān péi niǎn, qū gǔ zhèn yīng

【英译】Putting on high caps the officials accompanied the emperor and the queen behind their private two-wheel cart, as the carts were heading forward, and the ribbons on their caps were fluttering.

【今译】他们戴着高高的官帽，陪着皇帝皇后出游，驾着车马，帽带飘舞着，好不威风。

Lines 129 & 130
70. 世禄侈富，车驾肥轻

【拼音】shì lù chǐ fù, chē jià féi qīng

【英译】The posterities of their families would get paid in generations and they lived in extravagance; their carts were driven by stout and strong horses and their fir robes were light.

【今译】他们的子孙世代领受俸禄，奢侈豪富，出门时车豪华马肥壮，兽毛大衣轻盈暖和。

【说明】In ancient China the peerages were hereditary, so the posterities of a noble family would get benefits from the government and they didn't have to work. Line 130 is adopted from Paragraph 4 of Section 6 of *Analects of Confucius*.

在古代中国，爵位是世袭的。所以，贵族的后代可享受政府给的俸禄，自己不用工作。第130句引自《论语》第六章第四段。

Lines 131 & 132
71. 策功茂实，勒碑刻铭

【拼音】cè gōng mào shí, lè bēi kè míng.

【英译】Their achievements in both civil administration and military affairs were tremendous and real; their meritorious deeds will be carried in the inscriptions carved on stone tablets.

【今译】朝廷还翔实地记载了他们的功德，刻在碑石上流传后世。

Lines 133 & 134
72. 磻溪伊尹，佐时阿衡

【拼音】pán xī yī yǐn, zuǒ shí ā héng

【英译】The River Pan was where Jiang Shang became the Grand Tutor. Chef Yi Yin, having administered political affairs of the time, was given the title of A Heng.

【今译】周文王磻溪遇姜尚，尊他为"太公望"；伊尹辅佐时政，商汤王封伊尹为"阿衡"。

【说明】The River Pan was the place Jiang Shang（姜尚，with Ziya as his adult name）fished without any baits, and the fishing hook was 3.9 inches above the water. Passersby asked him if he could get any fish, and he answered that those who are willing to be caught will come to the hook.

磻溪是姜尚（字子牙）垂钓的地方。他的鱼钩上没有鱼食，且离水面有三寸高。过路的人问他如何能钓到鱼，他说愿者自会上钩。

Yi Yin was an orphan and grew up by the river side of "Yishui" —that's why his family name is "Yi". He was picked up by the servants of the Youshen family and raised up as a chef. After Youshen was married to Cheng Tang, the ruler of Shang, he naturally became the chef of the ruler. He purposely made poor taste of the food until the ruler talked to him. He grasped the opportunity to tell the ruler about his views on the situation and how to further the advancement of the state. The ruler was surprised and happy and appointed him as the Prime Minister. He was thus able to assist Cheng Tang to conquer the Xia Dynasty and ensured a nice beginning of the 554-year life span of the Shang Dynasty. A Heng is a title similar to a Prime Minister.

伊尹是个孤儿，在伊水旁长大，这是他姓伊的原因。有莘家族的奴仆收留了他，把他培养成一名厨师。随着有莘氏嫁给了成汤，伊尹也就成了成汤的厨师。他有意将饭菜做得很差，终于引来成汤与他谈话。他抓住机会，对成汤谈了他对时局的看法以及使国家兴盛的办法。成汤惊喜不已，任命伊尹为宰相。后来，伊尹帮助成汤征服了夏朝，并确保商朝为期554年的统治有了个好的开端。商朝的宰相叫阿衡。

Lines 135 & 136
73. 奄宅曲阜，微旦孰营

【拼音】yǎn zhái qū fù, wēi dàn shú yíng

【英译】To place one's residence at Qufu, only Dan, the Duke of Zhou deserved such a bounty.

【今译】只有周公旦才配得到古代奄国曲阜一带的封地，并在那里安家。

【说明】Dan's family name is Ji（姬）. He is the fourth son of King Wen of Zhou and the kid brother of King Wu of Zhou. He is the founder of China's traditional culture and a man of great accomplishment. He played a crucial role in establishing and consolidating the Zhou Dynasty. King Cheng was only a child when succeeded his father, who died of illness, and the

Duke had to be the regent to look after state affairs. However, there were rumors saying that the Duke wanted to usurp the state power. Some forces joined hands in rebellion at this juncture, so the Duke had to use three years to wipe out the rebellion. He regulated much protocol procedures and achieved much in music. In order not to lose any talents, he had to stop three times when washing his hair to see visitors, and it was said sometimes his meal was interrupted a few times by visitors. Once the young king was very ill, the Duke worried so much he even wrote in one of the prayers that he wished he could die for his nephew. The Duke handed over the power to the young king after he had been the regent for 7 years, yet he had to run away because the king didn't trust him. He was welcome back only when the king found in the archive the Duke's prayer and was much touched. He exerted all his efforts in the services to the state. He was given Qufu to build his residence. Qufu later became the capital of the State of Lu, and it was also the birth place of the Yellow Emperor. We could say the culture of the Zhou originated from there. The Duke was the founder and epitome of that culture. It is in this context that people say, aside from the Duke, who else is qualified to possess that place?

旦姓姬,是周文王的第四个儿子,是周武王的弟弟。他是中国传统文化的创建者,是建立了丰功伟业的人。他对周朝的建立和巩固起了关键的作用。周武王因病去世后,周成王继位,但他还是个孩子。周公不得不摄政,管理国家事务。但是,有谣言说他要夺权,甚至有人还联合起来造反。周公花了三年的时间平息叛乱。他建立了礼制,在音乐上也获得很多成绩。为了不使人才丢失,他洗头时不得不中断三次接见来访者;有时,他吃饭也会被打断几次。一次,年轻的皇帝得了病,周公非常担心,他在祷告词中写道,他宁愿替他的侄子去死。周公摄政七年后,将权力归还给成王。之后,他不得不逃亡,因为成王不相信他。后来,成王发现了周公写的祷告词,非常感动,就将周公接回了皇室。由于他对周朝忠心竭力,成王将曲阜赠给他做居住地。曲阜是黄帝的出生地,后来成了鲁国的都城。我们可以说,周的文化源自曲阜一带。周公就是此文化的奠基人和象征。也正是从这点出发,人们说,除了周公还有谁有资格占有(曲阜)这个地方呢?

Lines 137 & 138
74. 桓公匡合,济弱扶倾

【拼音】huán gōng kuāng hé, jì ruò fú qīng

【英译】Duke Huan brought order back to the land and

united with other dukes; he was able to do so because he helped the weak states and supported the falling empire.

【今译】桓公恢复了天下的秩序，团结了其他诸侯；他能这么做是由于他援助势单力薄的诸侯小国，并维护失去权威的周朝帝王。

【说明】Duke Huan of the State of Qi, assisted by his Prime Minister Guan Zhong（管仲）, developed his state into the most powerful one at the time. He was able to call nine meetings with other dukes and reached covenant with them. The empire of the Zhou Dynasty only existed in name, yet to support such an empire was something nobody would object.

齐桓公在他的宰相管仲的帮助下，将齐国发展成最强大的国家。他召集其他诸侯开过九次会，并与他们订立了盟约。这时，周王朝只是名义上存在；但是，若提出支持周王朝，诸侯中是没有人会反对的。

Lines 139 & 140
75. 绮回汉惠，说感武丁

【拼音】qǐ huí hàn huì, yuè gǎn wǔ dīng

【英译】The position of the Crown Prince of King Hui of

Han was secured by Qi Liji; inspired by his dream, Wu Ding used Fu Yue as his Prime Minister.

【今译】汉惠帝做太子时靠绮里季才幸免废黜，商君武丁感梦而得贤相傅说。

【说明】Liu Ying（刘盈），the son of Queen Lü, was the Crown Prince, yet weak-minded; Emperor Liu Bang wanted to appoint another son, whose mother was Mme Qi（戚夫人），to be the Crown Prince. Hearing this, Queen Lü asked the famous Four White to be tutors of the Crown Prince. Because of this move, the emperor was not able to remove Liu Ying. After the emperor passed away, the Queen was very cruel to Mme Qi and had her legs and arms cut off. Seeing the inhuman deeds of his mother, the new emperor was never happy and he died at the age of 23.

刘盈是吕后的儿子，当了太子，但是他生性懦弱。汉高帝刘邦想立另外一个儿子为太子，这个孩子是戚夫人生的。吕后听说这个消息，就找来商山四皓当刘盈的老师。这样一来，刘邦就放弃了换掉刘盈的想法。刘邦死后，吕后对戚夫人极其残酷，她砍掉了戚夫人的双腿和双手。看到母亲如此残暴，年轻的皇帝始终不开心，23岁时就去世了。

Wu Ding was the 22nd emperor of the Shang Dynasty. Fu

Yue was a slave, yet most capable and intelligent. In order to persuade his officials to agree to the appointment of Fu Yue, the emperor said he found a person in his dream who could contribute immensely to the royal court and he described where the person was and how he looked like. The superstitious officials found Fu Yue, and he became the Prime Minister. Fu Yue didn't let down the emperor. Fu Yue is still being remembered today, and people still go and visit his tomb and temple in today's Shanxi Province.

武丁是商朝第 22 位皇帝。傅说是一个奴隶，但是机智过人，而且能力非凡。为了说服他的大臣们同意起用傅说，武丁说他在梦里发现了一个人才，这个人会对皇室做出巨大的贡献，武丁还讲了此人在何处和他的长相。迷信的大臣们找到了傅说，傅说就这样当上了宰相。傅说没有让他的皇帝失望。人们如今仍然在纪念傅说。在山西省仍保留着傅说墓和傅说庙供人凭吊。

Lines 141 & 142
76. 俊乂密勿，多士寔宁

【拼音】jùn yì mì wù, duō shì shí níng

【英译】Talents all worked diligently; owing to the efforts of these capable men, the state is safe and peaceful.

【今译】能人治政勤勉努力,全靠许多这样的贤士,国家才安宁。

【说明】A talent chosen from among one thousand is called a "俊, jun"; a talent chosen from among one hundred is called a "乂, yi".

从一千人中选出的人才叫"俊",从百人中选出的人才叫"乂"。

Lines 143 & 144
77. 晋楚更霸,赵魏困横

【拼音】jìn chǔ gēng bà, zhào wèi kùn héng

【英译】King Wen of Jin and King Zhuang of Chu took turns in making their states the dominating powers; States of Zhao and Wei were baffled by the horizontal alliance.

【今译】晋文公和楚庄王先后当上了霸主,赵、魏两国因连横而受困于秦。

【说明】The adult name of King Wen of Jin is Chong'er(重耳). He took refuge in other countries for 19 years. By the time he came to the throne with the help of Duke Mu of Qin, he had been already 62 years old. In 632 B.C. State of Jin defeated the State of Chu and made the State of Jin a dominating state. Chu troops defeated the Jin troops in 597 B.C. And in the winter of 594 B.C., at a meeting of the 14 states, King Zhuang of Chu was elected the head of their alliance.

晋文公名重耳,在外逃亡19年。他在秦穆公的帮助下夺回王位时已经62岁了。公元前632年,晋国击败了楚国,而后在诸侯国中称霸。公元前597年,楚军击溃了晋军。公元前594年的冬天,楚庄王召集了14个诸侯国的会议,在会上,他被选为诸侯国联盟的盟主。

The policy of "horizontal alliance" was proposed by Zhang Yi（张仪）for the State of Qin. The key point in this policy was to make friends with states which were far away and attack states nearby one by one. This policy was pinpointed to the policy of "vertical integration" tailored up by Su Qin（苏秦）for the six states to guard against the State of Qin in the Warring States period. Because both Zhao and Wei were nearby states of Qin, they became the first prey of "horizontal alliance".

张仪为秦国提出了"连横"的策略。这个策略的关键是远交近攻。此策略与苏秦为战国时期六国联合抗秦提出的

"合纵"策略针锋相对。由于赵国和魏国是秦国的近邻,它们就成了"连横"策略的最早的牺牲品。

Lines 145 & 146
78. 假途灭虢,践土会盟

【拼音】jiǎ tú miè guó, jiàn tǔ huì méng

【英译】The State of Jin borrowed road from the State of Yu for purpose of conquering the State of Guo; Duke Wen of Jin came into alliance with other dukes at Jiantu.

【今译】晋国向虞国借路去消灭虢国,晋文公在践土与诸侯会盟。

【说明】The record of this event could be found in *The Spring and Autumn Annals with Zuo's Comment*. The State of Yu(虞) and the State of Guo(虢) were neighbors. When the State of Jin made the request of borrowing the road, one important official in the State of Yu, Gong Zhiqi saw through the plot and asked his King not to let out the road to Jin. But the King didn't take his advice. After Jin conquered the State of Guo, they also wiped out the State of Yu on their way back.

《春秋左传》对此事件有记载。虞国比邻虢国。当晋国提出向虞国借路时，大夫宫之奇识破了晋国的阴谋，劝国君不要答应借路。但是，虞国国君没有听取宫的意见。晋国在消灭了虢国后，在回师的路上，也把虞国灭了。

After the State of Jin defeated the State of Chu, Duke Wen of Jin called a meeting of all the dukes at Jiantu, where they came into an alliance with blood pledges.

晋国打败了楚国后，晋文公在践土这个地方召开了一次诸侯大会，与会的诸侯宣誓结盟。

Lines 147 & 148
79. 何遵约法，韩弊烦刑

【拼音】hé zūn yuē fǎ, hán bì fán xíng

【英译】Xiao He formulated laws for the Han Dynasty in a concise way; Han Fei died in the onerous criminal law he formulated himself.

【今译】萧何遵循简约刑法的精神制定九律，韩非却死于自己所制定的烦苛的刑法。

【说明】Xiao He（萧何）was an important member in Liu Bang's team and the first Prime Minister of Han. After Liu Bang's troops took the capital of Qin, some were busy

69

collecting wealth, some lost no time in collecting palace maids and had affairs with them. Xiao He was the only exception; he hurried to the office of the Prime Minister of Qin, where he collected all household registration, documents of topography, laws and decrees. All these data served as basic foundation for later policy-making and new legislations. Xiao He is also known in the story of "chasing after Han Xin in the moonlight". Han was a military master, serving in the troops of Liu Bang's rival, yet he was not given much importance, and then he came to work for Liu Bang, who appointed him as a petty officer looking after logistics. Again, he was disappointed and he left the barracks one night. Hearing about his leave, Xiao He immediately went out to chase Han. Having caught up with him, Xiao said if Liu Bang failed to put him on the right position, he would leave as well with Han. Xiao He then talked to Liu Bang, who agreed to appoint Han the Generalissimo of his troops, and a terrace was built especially for the appointment ceremony. Han Xin deserved such an honor; he finally wiped out all of the forces of Liu Bang's rivals and made it possible for the establishment of the Han Dynasty.

萧何是汉朝的第一任宰相。刘邦的军队拿下秦都后,有人搜刮财物,有人搜罗宫女,满足他们的肉欲。唯独萧何,进入秦都后，赶往秦丞相府，将秦朝有关国家户籍、地形、法令等资料统统收藏起来。这些资料对日后制定政策、法律提供了可靠的根据。人们知道萧何，还因为他"月下追韩信"的故事。韩信原在刘邦政敌那里，是天下无双的军事家，但是得不到重用，于是投到刘邦麾下。起初，刘邦让他当一个管理粮草的小官，韩信大失所望。韩信见在刘邦处仍不受重用，便在一个夜晚离开了汉营。萧何得知后，立即追赶韩信。追上后，萧何说如果刘邦不重用韩信，他就与韩信一起离开。萧何说服了刘邦，刘邦任命韩信为大将军，并专门修了一个高台，举行了拜将仪式。韩信也当得起这样的仪式，他带领刘邦的军队歼灭了敌军，使汉朝的建立成为可能。

Han Fei（韩非，appr. 280 B.C. – 233 B.C.）was the representative of the Legalist school, whose platform was to build a prosperous state with a powerful army and to run the state by law. He and Li Si（李斯）were all disciples of Xunzi（荀子）. The first emperor of Qin, having read such books written by Han Fei as *Indignation of the Lonely* and *Five Kinds of Men*, appreciated very much the ideas contained in the books and wanted very much to meet Han Fei in person. When Han Fei finally appeared before him, he placed Han at important posts and asked him to formulate laws for the empire. Li Si envied him and tried to frame him. Han finally died in prison, or to be exact, he died in the onerous law he formulated himself.

韩非(约公元前280—前233)是法家的代表人物。法家主张富国强兵、以法治国。韩非和李斯都是荀子的学生。秦始皇读过韩非所著的《孤愤》和《五蠹》,非常欣赏书中的观点,非常想见到韩非。当韩非终于出现在他面前时,他重用了韩非,让他为秦朝制定法律。李斯很嫉妒他,设法加害于他。最后,韩非死在牢狱里。或者,准确地说,他死于自己制定的烦苛的法律。

Lines 149 & 150
80. 起翦颇牧,用军最精

【拼音】qǐ jiǎn pō mù, yòng jūn zuì jīng

【英译】Generals of Qin are Bai Qi and Wang Jian; the generals of Zhao are Lian Po and Li Mu; they were most at home at matters of war.

【今译】秦将白起、王翦,赵将廉颇、李牧,最善于用兵。

【说明】Bai Qi（白起，? - 257 B.C.）has been ranked number one among all generals of the Warring States period. He joined the army at the age of 16. He took part in about 70 battles, never losing any of them. Wang Jian（王翦）was also a general of the State of Qin. He was the one who not only took the capital city of the State of Zhao, but also conquered the States of Zhao, Yan and Chu, and played a key role in unifying the entire country. When Lian Po（廉颇）was commanding troops, the State of Zhao suffered very few defeats. Li Mu（李牧，? - 229 B.C.）guarded Zhao's border successfully against the Huns. The above four are regarded as the most famous generals in the Warring States period.

在战国时期的将领中，白起（? —公元前257）是最了不起的。他16岁参军，经历了70多场战斗，未败过一次。王翦系秦国又一将领，他征服了赵、燕、楚三国，在统一国家中起到了重要作用。廉颇当军队统帅时，赵国很少吃败仗。李牧（? —公元前229）是赵国镇守边关、抗击匈奴的名将。上述四位都是战国时期的名将。

Lines 151 & 152
81. 宣威沙漠，驰誉丹青

【拼音】xuān wēi shā mò, chí yù dān qīng

【英译】The names and prestige of these generals went far to the northern desert; their reputation and portraits have got down to the record in history to be remembered for ever.

【今译】这些将领的声威远传到沙漠边地，美誉和画像一起流芳后世。

Lines 153 & 154
82. 九州禹迹，百郡秦并

【拼音】jiǔ zhōu yǔ jì, bǎi jùn qín bìng

【英译】Da Yu left his foot prints in all the nine regions when harnessing flood; the State of Qin annexed a hundred prefectures.

【今译】九州处处留有大禹治水的足迹，全国各郡在秦并六国后归于统一。

【说明】Da Yu（大禹）was the last beneficiary of the abdicating system and became the next ruler. His son Qi（启）succeeded him and began the family hereditary of state power. However, this was not the fault of Da Yu. The decision was not made by himself and there was no one else qualified. Da Yu was a good king. Confucius said he could not find anything not proper in him. He left home only four days after his wedding, and he was away from home for thirteen years to fight against flood. He passed by home three times, and each time he didn't get in. "Nine regions" was another way of saying "the entire country".

大禹是禅让制度的最后一位受益人,他继承了舜的王位。他的权力由他的儿子启接替,开始了国家权力家族的传续。但这不是大禹本人的过错,决定不是他做出的。那时,没有合适的人选。大禹是个好君主。孔子说他在大禹身上找不出什么毛病。他婚后第四天就离家去治水了。他治水 13 年,三过家门而不入。九州是指全国的领土。

Qin unified the entire country. In the pre-Qin period, a prefecture was smaller than a county. In the Tang Dynasty a prefecture was the largest administrative unit. The county heads in the Qin Dynasty were directly appointed by the central government and they were responsible to the central government. It should be pointed out here that the introduction of the "County System" in the Qin Dynasty was of great historical importance. It marked a transition from the duke fiefdom to the bureaucratic political system of centralization of authority in ancient China.

秦统一了全国。在先秦时期郡比县小。在唐朝郡是最大的行政单位。在秦朝，县令是由朝廷任命的，要对朝廷负责。需要指出的是，"郡县制"的启用是具有重要历史意义的，它标志着古代中国由诸侯分封制过渡到了中央集权的官僚政治制度。

Lines 155 & 156
83. 岳宗泰岱，禅主云亭

【拼音】yuè zōng tài dài, shàn zhǔ yún tíng

【英译】Mount Tai was the most prestigious among the Five Sacred Mountains in China; the ceremony of offering sacrifice for the earth took place at Yunyunshan and Tingtingshan at the foot of Mount Tai.

【今译】五岳中人们最尊崇东岳泰山，历代帝王都在泰山脚下的云云山和亭亭山举行封禅活动。

【说明】The other four of the Sacred Mountains are

Hengshan（衡山），Huashan（华山），Northern Hengshan（恒山）and Songshan（嵩山）. Mount Tai locates in the middle part of Shandong Province with total area of 426 square kilometers. Mount Tai was called Daizong in the ancient time. The Chinese character "岱" pronounces as "dai" has been used exclusively as another name of Mount Tai since the Spring and Autumn period. It is also referred to as Dongyue（the Sacred Mountain of east China）. In 1987, Mount Tai was listed as Cultural and Natural World Heritage site by UNESCO and honored "World Geopark" in 2006. In China, Mount Tai is among the first group of "National Parks", the state 5A-class tourist attractions, the National Most Decent Spots in China.

其他四座山是衡山、华山、恒山和嵩山。泰山位于山东省中部，占地426平方公里。泰山在远古时期被称为岱宗，春秋时期以来"岱"字就专指泰山；泰山也被称为东岳（意为中国东部的圣山）。1987年，联合国教科文组织正式批准把泰山风景名胜列入世界文化遗产和自然遗产清单。2006年，它被授予"世界地质公园"的称号。泰山是中国第一批国家级风景名胜区、5A级旅游景区和全国文明风景旅游区之一。

The ceremony of offering sacrifice to the earth was called "禅，shan"; the ceremony of offering sacrifice to the heaven was called "封，feng", which would normally take place on Mount Tai.

祭地的礼仪叫"禅"，祭祀上天的活动叫"封"，"封"通常都会在泰山举行。

Lines 157 & 158
84. 雁门紫塞，鸡田赤城

【拼音】yàn mén zǐ sài, jī tián chì chéng

【英译】Yanmen is the famous pass on the northern frontier; the purple fortress is The Great Wall; Jitian is the remotest point of official postal relay on the northwest; Chicheng is a unique peak on the Tiantaishan.

【今译】名关有北疆雁门，要塞有万里长城，驿站有边地鸡田，奇山有天台赤城。

【说明】Literally Yanmen means the gate for the wild goose, and it is so named because it was the lowest point for wild geese to fly out to the other side of the mountain. Many hero generals in history went through this pass when fighting against the Huns. The Great Wall on the western end is on red soil, so it is also called the "purple fortress".

从字面上讲，雁门就是大雁之门。之所以如此命名，是因为此处是大雁可以飞过去的最低的地方。历史上有很多英雄的将领，出雁门关去抗击匈奴。长城西端的土壤是红色的，所以被称作紫塞。

Jitian was the oldest and remotest point of official postal relay. In ancient China documents and written orders were delivered on horseback through postal relay points all over the country. Literally Chicheng means red city, named after local soil. The peak in the red city area is over 300 meters high, a big contrast with green hills around it. Its morning rosy clouds are famous and have been considered as one of the eight major scenes in the area. Tiantaishan is also an important Buddhist site.

鸡田是最老、最远的驿站。在中国古代，文件和书面命令是通过在全国各地的驿站传递的。赤城字面上是"红色的城"的意思，它得名于当地土壤的颜色。其最高处300多米，与周围的绿色峰峦形成鲜明的对比。它清晨玫瑰色的云彩很出名，是当地的八景之一。天台山也是著名的佛教圣地。

Lines 159 & 160
85. 昆池碣石，巨野洞庭

【拼音】kūn chí jié shí, jù yě dòng tíng

【英译】To watch inland water one has to get to Dianchi Lake in Kunming; to view the sea one has to be at Jieshi Mountain; other lakes worth seeing are Juye in Shandong Province and Dongting in Hunan Province.

【今译】赏池需去昆明滇池，观海应赴河北碣石山，看泽应去山东巨野，望湖需上湖南洞庭。

【说明】Kunchi is the Dianchi Lake in Kunming, which is the sixth largest fresh water lake in China. The Jieshi Mountain stands by the seaside in Hebei Province; it is 695 meters above sea level and has been a spot to view sea scenery. Both the first emperor of Qin and Emperor Wu of Han toured this mountain, and Cao Cao composed a famous poem "Viewing the Blue Sea" when he was in this mountain. Cao Cao was a well-known statesman, military master, writer and calligrapher at the end of the Eastern Han period; he was the one who founded the Kingdom of Wei. Aside from his mastery of the art of war, his poems have been very influential.

昆池就是昆明的滇池。它是中国第六大淡水湖。碣石山位于河北省沿海地区,它海拔695米,是观看海景的好去处。秦始皇和汉武帝都到过此山。曹操在此山上还作过一首诗《观沧海》。曹操是东汉末年著名政治家、军事家、文学家和书法家,也是三国中曹魏政权的缔造者。曹操精兵法,善诗歌。

Juye Lake doesn't exist now, but it was a huge lake in the lower ranges of the Yellow River in Shandong Province. It was over 150 kilometers long and over 50 kilometers wide before the Sui Dynasty and Tang Dynasty. Because of the accumulation of silt over time, its area has been reduced, which is now called Dongping Lake. Dongting Lake is situated in the northern part of Hunan Province to the south of the Jingjiang River of the Changjiang River. It is the third largest lake in China, next only to Qinghai Lake and Poyang Lake. It is also the second largest fresh water lake. It also connects with lakes outside its boundaries and there are mountains in the lake with beautiful scenery.

巨野湖如今已不复存在。但是,隋唐之前,它是山东省黄河下游的一个巨大湖泊,这个大湖南北三百余里,东西一百余里;后来,由于泥土的淤积,其湖水面积缩减,成了今天的东平湖。洞庭湖位于中国湖南省北部,长江荆江河段以南,是中国第三大湖,仅次于青海湖、鄱阳湖,也是中国第二大淡水湖。洞庭湖湖外有湖,湖中有山,景色优美。

Lines 161 & 162
86. 旷远绵邈,岩岫杳冥

【拼音】kuàng yuǎn mián miǎo, yán xiù yǎo míng

【英译】The land of China is so vast and infinite; the high mountains and deep valleys are so majestic and grand.

【今译】中国的国土广袤无垠,名山奇谷幽深秀丽、气象万千。

小结

The above can be considered the third part of the *Verse*. It covers the country, its politics, civil and military figures and beautiful landscape.

以上是全篇的第三部分。它讨论了国情、政治、军民人物和风景。

Lines 163 & 164
87. 治本于农，务兹稼穑

【拼音】zhì běn yú nóng, wù zī jià sè

【英译】The basic thing in running a country well is to develop agriculture; a good job must be done in sowing and harvesting.

【今译】治国的根本在发展农业，必须努力做好播种和收获。

Lines 165 & 166
88. 俶载南亩，我艺黍稷

【拼音】chù zǎi nán mǔ, wǒ yì shǔ jì

【英译】A new round of farm work has been started on the sun-facing land, and what is to be sowed are corn and millet.

【今译】一年的农活又在朝南的田地里开始了，在地里种上玉米，又种上了小米。

Lines 167 & 168
89. 税熟贡新，劝赏黜陟

【拼音】shuì shú gòng xīn, quàn shǎng chù zhì

【英译】To submit freshly harvested grain as tax to the state; farmers were awarded or punished and officials were promoted or deposed according to their performance of farming.

【今译】收获季节，用刚熟的新谷缴纳税粮，百姓和官员按收税的情况得到奖励或处罚。

Lines 169 & 170
90. 孟轲敦素，史鱼秉直

【拼音】mèng kē dūn sù, shǐ yú bǐng zhí

【英译】Meng Ke adored simplicity; Shi Yu was honest and upright.

【今译】孟轲崇尚简洁，史官子鱼秉性刚直。

【说明】Meng Ke（appr. 372 B.C. - 289 B.C.), also

known as Mengzi or Mencius, is the most important successor to Confucius. His writings, as set forth in the *Book of Mencius*, has been highly esteemed in China for many centuries. He is often referred to as the "Second Sage".

孟轲（约公元前372—前289）就是孟子，是孔子最重要的传承人。他写的《孟子》很多世纪以来一直受到尊崇。他被称为"亚圣"。

Shi Yu, a peer of Confucius, was a high ranking official in the State of Wei（卫）. He was known for his straight forwardness in speaking up his mind without any consideration of what would happen to him afterwards.

史鱼是与孔子同时代的人物，是卫国的高官。他以正直敢谏闻名，不在乎个人的得失。

Lines 171 & 172
91. 庶几中庸，劳谦谨敕

【拼音】shù jī zhōng yōng, láo qiān jǐn chì

【英译】If one can act as the above two, he could almost be regarded as practicing the golden rule; one should also be diligent, modest, cautious and discreet.

【今译】做人能像上面两位，就差不多合乎中庸的标准了；达到中庸还需要做到勤奋、谦逊、谨慎、端正。

【说明】The golden rule is to do things in a proper way without going to extremes. This sense of centeredness is expressed in the Chinese classic in this way："When joy, anger, sorrow and pleasure have not yet arisen, it is called the 'Mean'（中，centeredness, equilibrium）. When they arise to their appropriate levels, it is called 'Harmony'（和）. The 'Mean' is the great root of all-under-heaven. 'Harmony' is the penetration of the way through all-under-heaven. When the 'Mean' and 'Harmony' are actualized, heaven and earth are in their proper positions, and myriad things are nourished."

中庸就是做事取中不偏，不走极端。这种执中的思想在中国的经典里是这样表达的："喜怒哀乐之未发谓之中；发而皆中节谓之和。中也者，天下之大本也；和也者，天下之达道也。致中和，天地位焉，万物育焉。"

Lines 173 & 174
92. 聆音察理，鉴貌辨色

【拼音】líng yīn chá lǐ, jiàn mào biàn sè

【英译】When you listen to somebody, you have to examine if what he says is correct; when you look at the appearance of others, you should tell if they're honest or crafty.

【今译】听别人说话，要仔细审察是否正确；看别人面色，要小心辨析他是忠还是奸。

Lines 175 & 176
93. 贻厥嘉猷，勉其祗植

【拼音】yí jué jiā yóu, miǎn qí zhī zhí

【英译】The best thing to leave to the posterity is a piece of good advice; posterities should be asked to be prudent and try to establish themselves.

【今译】给后人留下最珍贵的莫过于正确高明的忠告，应勉励后人谨慎小心地处世立身。

Lines 177 & 178
94. 省躬讥诫，宠增抗极

【拼音】xǐng gōng jī jiè, chǒng zēng kàng jí

【英译】When you hear derision and admonishment, you should examine yourself; excessive affection may lead to the opposite extreme.

【今译】听到别人的讥讽告诫,要反省自身;备受恩宠然后得意忘形,会走向反面。

Lines 179 & 180
95. 殆辱近耻,林皋幸即

【拼音】dài rǔ jìn chǐ, lín gāo xìng jí

【英译】When insult and shame will fall on you, you should retire from your post and go into forest and lakes in the hills, and you could then escape from troubles.

【今译】知道有危险或耻辱的事快要发生时,还是归隐山林为好。

Lines 181 & 182
96. 两疏见机,解组谁逼

【拼音】liǎng shū jiàn jī, jiě zǔ shuí bī

【英译】The two Shus chose a right time to retire; nobody forced them to untie their official belts.

【今译】疏广、疏受是因为预见到危患的苗头才告老还乡，而不是有人逼迫他们辞官。

【说明】The two Shus are Shu Guang (疏广) and Shu Shou (疏受), who were an uncle and his nephew, both tutors of the Crown Prince of the Han Dynasty. They taught for years and then retired, because their position was very much envied by others.

两疏是指疏广和疏受叔侄俩。他们都是汉朝太子的老师。他们教太子读书，然后辞职，因为他们的职务很容易招人妒忌。

Lines 183 & 184
97. 索居闲处，沉默寂寥

【拼音】suǒ jū xián chǔ, chén mò jì liáo

【英译】To live by oneself and pass days in leisure, one can thus enjoy tranquility, not having to talk about who is right or wrong.

【今译】离群独居，悠闲度日，整天不用多费唇舌，清静无为岂不是好事。

Lines 185 & 186
98. 求古寻论，散虑逍遥

【拼音】qiú gǔ xún lùn, sàn lù xiāo yáo

【英译】One can find pleasure in questing for ancient events and figures or read axioms and aphorism; in doing so, one can get rid of all worries and be entirely idle and free.

【今译】想想古人的事，翻翻古人的书，消去往日的忧虑，乐得逍遥自在。

Lines 187 & 188
99. 欣奏累遣，戚谢欢招

【拼音】xīn zòu lèi qiǎn, qī xiè huān zhāo

【英译】Deliver things delightful and throw away boredom and encumbrance; having thrown away annoyance, one can enjoy rapture and glee.

【今译】将轻松的事凑到一起，把费力的事丢在一边，消除不尽的烦恼，得来无限的快乐。

Lines 189 & 190
100. 渠荷的历，园莽抽条

【拼音】qú hé dì lì, yuán mǎng chōu tiáo

【英译】The lotus in the pond is so splendid; new sprouts are coming out of the grass and woods in the garden.

【今译】池里的荷花开得光润鲜艳，园中的草木抽出条条嫩枝。

【说明】In Chinese culture, lotus is something auspicious. Confucian scholars regard it as a gentleman among various flowers.

中国文化视莲花为吉祥物。儒家学者视它为花中君子。

Lines 191 & 192
101. 枇杷晚翠，梧桐蚤凋

【拼音】pí pa wǎn cuì, wú tóng zǎo diāo

【英译】The loquat tree remains green even in winter; the Chinese parasol tree withers as soon as autumn comes.

【今译】枇杷树到了岁晚还是苍翠欲滴，梧桐树刚刚入秋就早早地凋谢了。

Lines 193 & 194
102. 陈根委翳，落叶飘摇

【拼音】chén gēn wěi yì, luò yè piāo yáo

【英译】Trees with old roots are withered and collapsed; the falling leaves are fluttering in the air.

【今译】陈根老树枯萎倒伏，落叶在风中四处飘荡。

Lines 195 & 196
103. 游鹍独运，凌摩绛霄

【拼音】yóu kūn dú yùn, líng mó jiàng xiāo

【英译】The wandering crane is on its flight alone, dashing up to the purple clouds high in the sky.

【今译】自由自在翱翔的鹍鸡，直冲布满彩霞的云霄。

Lines 197 & 198
104. 耽读玩市，寓目囊箱

【拼音】dān dú wán shì, yù mù náng xiāng

【英译】Being fully immersed in his studies in the book store in the noisy market, what could catch his sight were only books and bookcases.

【今译】在街市上的书店里沉迷于读书，能够引起他注意的只有书籍和书箱。

【说明】The person who did so was Wang Chong（王充，27 - appr. 97）, a philosopher in the Eastern Han. His works *On Scaling*（《论衡》）is one of the most important books in the history of Chinese philosophy.

这个故事说的是东汉哲学家王充（公元27—约97）。他所著的《论衡》是中国哲学史上一部很重要的著作。

Lines 199 & 200
105. 易輶攸畏，属耳垣墙

【拼音】yì yóu yōu wèi, zhǔ ěr yuán qiáng

【英译】Be on guard against thoughtless remarks; beware of the eavesdroppers, even if you're alone in the room.

【今译】要警惕轻忽的言论，即便空无一人，也要提防隔墙有耳。

Lines 201 & 202
106. 具膳餐饭，适口充肠

【拼音】jù shàn cān fàn, shì kǒu chōng cháng

【英译】Our food includes meat and grain; they should be tasty and allay one's hunger.

【今译】膳食中应有粮食和肉食，既能合口味，又能吃饱。

Lines 203 & 204
107. 饱饫烹宰，饥厌糟糠

【拼音】bǎo yù pēng zǎi, jī yàn zāo kāng

【英译】When one is full, slaughter a chicken or cooking a fish would seem redundant; when one is hungry, husks and chaff are good food.

【今译】饱的时候就不愿意去宰鸡烹鱼了，饿的时候糠谷也是好的食品。

Lines 205 & 206
108. 亲戚故旧，老少异粮

【拼音】qīn qi gù jiù, lǎo shào yì liáng

【英译】Relatives are to be treated with warmth; food prepared for the old and the young should be different from yours.

【今译】亲属、朋友会面要盛情款待，老人、小孩的食物应有所不同。

Lines 207 & 208
109. 妾御绩纺，侍巾帏房

【拼音】qiè yù jì fǎng, shì jīn wéi fáng

【英译】Women should do a good job of housework, and wait on their husbands with great care.

95

【今译】妇女要管理好家务，尽心恭敬地服侍好丈夫。

Lines 209 & 210
110. 纨扇圆絜，银烛炜煌

【拼音】wán shàn yuán jié, yín zhú wěi huáng

【英译】The girl's round fan made of white silk is kept clean; the silver white candle is so bright and brilliant.

【今译】绢制的团扇又圆又洁净，银色的烛台上烛火辉煌。

Lines 211 & 212
111. 昼眠夕寐，蓝笋象床

【拼音】zhòu mián xī mèi, lán sǔn xiàng chuáng

【英译】A good way of life would include a nap in the day and a sound sleep at night; sleeping on a soft bamboo mat in the bed decorated with ivory is really desirable.

【今译】过好日子就要白日小憩，晚上就寝，用青篾编成的竹席和象牙雕饰的床榻就更好了。

Lines 213 & 214
112. 弦歌酒宴，接杯举觞

【拼音】xián gē jiǔ yàn, jiē bēi jǔ shāng

【英译】A good life also includes a banquet amid singing and playing of string instruments, raising cups to drink to one's content.

【今译】过好日子还要奏着乐，唱着歌，摆酒开宴，接过酒杯，开怀畅饮。

Lines 215 & 216
113. 矫手顿足，悦豫且康

【拼音】jiǎo shǒu dùn zú, yuè yù qiě kāng

【英译】People at such a time would wave their hands in rhythm and stamp the beat with their foot; they are indeed joyful, peaceful and healthy.

【今译】情不自禁地手舞足蹈，真是又快乐又安康。

Lines 217 & 218
114. 嫡后嗣续，祭祀烝尝

【拼音】dí hòu sì xù, jì sì zhēng cháng

【英译】To carry on the family line from generations to generations, great care is needed when offering sacrifices in the four seasons.

【今译】子孙一代代传承，一年四季的祭祀大礼不能马虎。

【说明】The responsibility of carrying on the family was normally placed on the son of the wife, not children of concubines. The sacrifice offered to the heaven was called "祭, ji" while that offered to the earth was called "祀, si".

传宗接代的责任主要靠正妻的儿子来完成，而不是靠妾的儿子。祭天叫"祭"，祭地叫"祀。"

Lines 219 & 220
115. 稽颡再拜，悚惧恐惶

【拼音】qǐ sǎng zài bài, sǒng jù kǒng huáng

【英译】To bow once and again, one should kneel down and touch the ground with one's forehead; one should also be deferential when doing the offering.

【今译】跪着磕头，拜了再拜；礼仪要周全恭敬，态度要虔诚。

Lines 221 & 222
116. 笺牒简要，顾答审详

【拼音】jiān dié jiǎn yào, gù dá shěn xiáng

【英译】Letters to others should be concise; prudence and details are needed when answering others' questions.

【今译】给别人写信要简明扼要，回答别人问题要详细周全。

【说明】"笺，jian" is a letter-head; "牒，die" is bamboo slips. It means "letters" when the two characters are used together.

"笺"指信笺，"牒"指竹简。两个字在一起用时就是信函的意思。

Lines 223 & 224
117. 骸垢想浴，执热愿凉

【拼音】hái gòu xiǎng yù, zhí rè yuàn liáng

【英译】Take a shower after you have made yourself dirty; you wish the temperature could go down when you can hardly put up with the heat.

【今译】身上有了污垢就想洗澡，暑热难耐就希望天变凉。

Lines 225 & 226
118. 驴骡犊特，骇跃超骧

【拼音】lǘ luó dú tè, hài yuè chāo xiāng

【英译】Donkeys, mules, calves and cows are not good at running, yet they leap higher than horses when being terrified.

【今译】驴骡牛儿不善跑，受惊一跃超马奔。

【说明】The lines stress the importance of safety and care when raising a family.

这两句话强调居家时安全和互相关心的重要性。

Lines 227 & 228
119. 诛斩贼盗，捕获叛亡

【拼音】zhū zhǎn zéi dào, bǔ huò pàn wáng

【英译】Bandits and thieves must be seriously punished; rebels and ruffians must be captured by the government.

【今译】对抢劫、偷窃、反叛、逃亡的人要严厉惩罚，该抓的抓。

Lines 229 & 230
120. 布射僚丸，嵇琴阮啸

【拼音】bù shè liáo wán, jī qín ruǎn xiào

【英译】Lü Bu was good at archery and Xiong Yiliao was a master of slingshot; Ji Kang was known for his lute playing and Ruan Ji was able to shout for a long time.

【今译】吕布擅长射箭，熊宜僚有射弹弓的绝活；嵇康善于弹琴，阮籍能撮口长啸。

【说明】Lü Bu（吕布，? - 199）was a famous general in late Eastern Han period; Xiong Yiliao（熊宜僚）was a warrior of the State of Chu in the Spring and Autumn period.

布指吕布（？—199），东汉末期的名将；熊宜僚是春秋时楚国的勇士。

Ji Kang（嵇康）was a writer and musician in the Kingdom of Wei in the Three-Kingdom period; Ruan Ji（阮籍）was a poet in the Kingdom of Wei in the Three-Kingdom period.

嵇康是三国时魏国的文学家和音乐家，阮籍是三国时魏国的诗人。

Lines 231 & 232
121. 恬笔伦纸，钧巧任钓

【拼音】tián bǐ lún zhǐ, jūn qiǎo rén diào

【英译】Meng Tian invented the brush pen; Cai Lun invented paper; Ma Jun invented waterwheel; Mr. Ren was famous for fishing.

【今译】蒙恬造笔，蔡伦造纸，马钧巧制水车，任公子善钓大鱼。

【说明】Meng Tian (蒙恬，？- 210 B.C.) was a general of the State of Qin; Cai Lun (蔡伦，appr. 62 - 121) was an eunuch of the royal court of the Eastern Han period and the inventor of paper making.

蒙恬（？—公元前210）是秦国的大将；蔡伦（约公元62—121）是东汉皇宫里的太监，发明了造纸术。

Ma Jun (马钧) was an inventor in the Three-Kingdom period; according to Zhuangzi, when Mr. Ren caught a huge fish he used 50 cows as his baits.

钧指马钧，他是三国时期的发明家；任指任公子，庄子说他用50头牛做鱼饵钓上了一条大鱼。

Lines 233 & 234
122. 释纷利俗，并皆佳妙

【拼音】shì fēn lì sú, bìng jiē jiā miào

【英译】The skills and techniques of these people could either dissolve disputes among people or bring good to the society; these superb and ingenious skills have won warm acclaim from the people.

【今译】他们的技艺有的解人纠纷,有的方便民众,都高明巧妙,为人称道。

Lines 235 & 236
123. 毛施淑姿,工颦妍笑

【拼音】máo shī shū zī, gōng pín yán xiào

【英译】Both Mao Qiang and Xi Shi were famous beauties of China; they looked pretty even when they frown and their smiles were charming.

【今译】毛嫱、西施都是中国有名的美女;哪怕是皱着眉头,她们的模样也很美而且她们的笑容很有魅力。

【说明】Mao Qiang(毛嫱)and Xi Shi(西施)were famous beauties of the State of Yue in the Spring and Autumn period.

毛嫱和西施是春秋时越国的美女。

Lines 237 & 238
124. 年矢每催,曦晖朗曜

【拼音】nián shǐ měi cuī, xī huī lǎng yào

【英译】Youth can be gone very quickly and time always tries to age people, while only the sun can shine forever in the sky.

【今译】可惜青春易逝,岁月匆匆催人渐老,只有太阳的光辉永远朗照。

Lines 239 & 240
125. 璇玑悬斡,晦魄环照

【拼音】xuán jī xuán wò, huì pò huán zhào

【英译】The ladle of the Big Dipper changes its direction in each season; the moon casts its light to all corners of the human world.

【今译】高悬的北斗七星随着四季变换转动,皎洁的月光洒遍人间每个角落。

Lines 241 & 242
126. 指薪修祜,永绥吉劭

【拼音】zhǐ xīn xiū hù, yǒng suí jí shào

【英译】When wood burns, fire can last; one should

cultivate himself and accumulate his happiness in order to pass on the kindling. The posterities can enjoy forever a stable and peaceful life.

【今译】薪柴会燃烧成灰,火焰确能永存。行善积德才能像薪尽火传那样精神长存,子孙也可享福禄安康。

【说明】It implies that a person's flesh would disappear, yet life always exists.

其含义为一个人的肉体可以消失,但精神是永存的。

Lines 243 & 244
127. 矩步引领,俯仰廊庙

【拼音】jǔ bù yǐn lǐng, fǔ yǎng láng miào

【英译】In life one should stride with his head up in big steps; one should also be serious and cautious as if attending a ceremony in the temple.

【今译】在生活里要昂头迈步,也要像参加庙里的大礼那样严肃和谨慎。

Lines 245 & 246
128. 束带矜庄，徘徊瞻眺

【拼音】shù dài jīn zhuāng, pái huái zhān tiào

【英译】One should be neatly dressed and look solemn; one should also be cautious and prudent, look far ahead and aim high.

【今译】要注重整束衣冠，庄重从容、高瞻远望。

Lines 247 & 248
129. 孤陋寡闻，愚蒙等诮

【拼音】gū lòu guǎ wén, yú méng děng qiào

【英译】My knowledge is so limited and I am poorly informed about the world, and my foolish self is waiting for others to question and mock me.

【今译】我学识浅陋，见闻有限，愚昧的我只好等人们对我的责问和嘲笑了。

Lines 249 & 250
130. 谓语助者，焉哉乎也

【拼音】Wèi yǔ zhù zhě, yān zāi hū yě

【英译】All I know are some auxiliary words, such as "to, of, oh and wow".

【今译】我所知道的仅仅是"焉、哉、乎、也"这几个语气助词。

I have tried my best to polish it with some paraphrasing, to make it read more or less like a poem below.

我尽力对译文进行修饰，有些地方甚至进行了意译，尽量让它读起来像一首诗。

The Verse of One Thousand Characters（without annotations）
《千字文》（无注释）

A

The earth is yellow and the sky is black,

The universe is huge and infinite.

A full sun and moon and their waning,

Stars are placed in the limitless sky shinning.

Winter comes and summer goes,

To harvest in autumn and to store up in winter in barns.

The epact has been accumulated into a month and is inserted into a leap year,

Ancient people used bamboo pipes to set tunes and to decide a weather marker.

The ascending clouds would become rain when contacting cold current,

In cold night dew would be condensed into frost.

Gold is produced in the Lijiang River,

Jade is produced in the Mount Kunlun area.

Behind the sword Ju Que are stories,

The pearl that was called Ye Guang also contain tales.

Plum and apple are best fruits,

Most important vegetables are ginger and leaf mustard.

Sea water is salty and river water is fresh,

Fish swims in the water and birds fly fast in the sky as a flash.

The Dragon Teacher and the Fire Emperor,

Bird Officer and Human Emperor were names of ancient rulers.

Chinese Characters were invented,

People began to put on cloths to have their bodies covered.

To give the throne and state power to others,

That happened in the Youyu and Taotang tribes.

To pacify people and punish the criminal and culprit,

Was what King Wu of Zhou and King Tang of Shang did.

They sat in their throne and asked officials about state affairs,

The state was peaceful and achievements were outstanding,

What they did was hanging up their gowns and folding their hands,

Aside from the above they did nothing.

They cared about the common folks,

Such tribes as Rong and Qiang bowed to them on knees.

The country was unified of places far and near,

People in the four seas were all subjects of the emperor.

Phoenixes are chirping happily in the bamboo forest,

White horses are eating grass in the field;

The rule by virtue had even touched grass and trees,

What had reached to everyone in every corner were benefits.

B

As far as our flesh and hair are concerned,

They resemble rudimentary affairs.

Caution is needed to take them with good care,

Never venture to harm them and your efforts not to spare.

Girls adore integrity and cleanness,

Boys imitate virtuous and talented persons.

Mistakes must be corrected when you are aware of them,

Do not give up when it is within thy realm.

Not to talk about the shortcomings of others,

Not to be conceited because of the strong points.

One's trustworthiness should stand tests,

It is difficult to measure one's magnanimities.

Mozi was sad when white silk threads dyed into another color,

The Book of Songs sings praises of a lamb's benign character.

People admire the virtue and behavior of capable persons,

They should also check their desires and follow suit of saints.

When virtue is fostered fame would come,

Fair carriage makes appearance respectable and solemn.

Sound goes far in an empty valley,

In a spacious hall voice can be heard very clearly.

Misfortune is caused by the accumulation of evil deeds,

Fortune is an outcome of prodigal benefactions.

A foot long piece of jade should not be regarded as a treasure,

Even a short span of time should be taken as a precious ware.

To look after the father and provide service to the King,

Take pains and be respectful in service.

Do your best in performing filial duties,

Be dedicated in the loyalty to the majesties.

Thou be careful when on thin ice and by an abyss,

Spare no efforts to ensure thine parents are well in all seasons.

Thine virtue should be as fragrant as orchid,

And as pine that is flourishing and stalwart.

When virtue reaches to posterities, it is like running water in the river,

Virtue of the progenitor is like deep running water, sound and clear.

Thine carriage should be in a serene and composed manner,

Thine words should sound definite, pacifying as a speaker.

A solid beginning is of course beautiful,

We should strive for a good ending as well.

Such is the basis for fame and achievement,

On such a base, thine fame and profession would be without limit.

Those whose studies are the best could be officials,

An official would thus perform duties and handle political matters.

Efforts have been made to keep alive the sweet crabapple tree,

The longer Count Shao of the Zhou Dynasty has left, the more people sing praises of him in their pray.

Music may vary according to the status of people, noble or humble,

Propriety to the lowly is different from that to the lofty.

Harmony between the young and the old is a priority,

One (very often the wife) would follow what the spouse (very often the husband) has proposed so lovely.

One should accept the instruction of teachers outside,

One should follow the norms of mother at home.

Treat your aunts and uncles like your parents with full attention,

Aunts and uncles should treat their nephews like their own children.

One should be most concerned with his brothers,

Because they breathe the same family air and are like branches on the same tree that have the same roots.

The friend who is congenial to you should be chosen,

A friend should be able to discuss studies with you and give you admonition.

A feeling of commiseration contains kindness and

affection,

In urgency such a feeling should be kept in consistency.

Integrity, justice, cleanness and modesty are indispensible,

Even at times of adversity.

A calm heart brings ease and comfort,

A restless heart would make thee exhausted.

A pure heart would fulfill thine aspirations,

Thy will would be altered if thou chase after material needs.

To persist in elegant integrity,

Thou would be automatically tied to a good luck and always be lucky.

C

The capital cities of ancient China are magnificent,

Sometimes the capital was in the east and other times it was in the west.

Luoyang has Mount Mang at its back and Luo River at its front,

River Wei is on the left side of Xi'an and River Jing is on its right side.

Palaces and halls seem to overlap each other on the winding roads,

People would be startled at the sight of the seemingly flying towers.

Birds and animals are painted on the walls of the palaces and halls,

There are also immortals and deities painted in colors.

The doors of auxiliary halls are also on the side,

The draperies are decorated with pearls, coral and precious jade.

Tables and seats are prepared for banquets,

Being played are string and pipe instruments.

The officials are climbing up the steps,

The jade inlaid on the caps of officials is glittering like stars.

To the right of the main hall is Guang Nei Hall, the Imperial Library,

Cheng Ming Hall to the left is where officials rest and kept fatigue away.

These are places where classic works are collected,

And places where heroes and talents are gathered.

There are Du Du's manuscript and Zhong Yao's calligraphy,

Characters written with resin and classics hidden in walls are also on display.

Civil and military officials were gathered in the hall,

The dukes and highest officials stood on both sides of the road, waiting for the emperor to call.

The fief granted to every highest official is as big as eight counties,

Each family was provided with over one thousand men as its guards.

Putting on high caps, the officials accompanied the emperor and the queen behind their private two-wheel cart,

The ribbons on their caps were fluttering, as the carts were heading forward.

The posterities of these families would get paid for generations and they all led an extravagant life,

Their carts were driven by stout and strong horses and their fir robes were light and attractive.

Their achievements in both civil administration and military affairs were tremendous and real,

Their meritorious deeds will be carried in the inscriptions carved on stone tablets as a memorial.

The River Pan was where Jiang Shang was found for services for the Zhou Dynasty and chef Yi Yin,

Having administered political affairs of the time, Chef Yi Yin was given the title of A Heng—the position of a Prime Minister in the period of Yin.

To place one's residence at Qufu,

Only Dan, the Duke of Zhou deserved to take such a move.

Duke Huan brought order back to the land and united with other dukes,

He did so because he supported the falling empire and helped the weak states.

The position of the Crown Prince of King Hui of Han was secured by Qi Liji,

Wu Ding, inspired by his dream, used Fu Yue as his Prime Minister, who was only a mason in the community.

Talents all worked diligently,

Owing to the efforts of them, the state was in peace and safety.

King Wen of Jin and King Zhuang of Chu took turns in making their states the dominating powers,

States of Zhao and Wei were baffled by the horizontal alliance proposed by a Qin officer.

The State of Jin borrowed road from the State of Yu for purpose of conquering the Guo State,

Duke Wen of Jin came into alliance at Jiantu with other dukes.

Xiao He formulated laws for the Han Dynasty in a concise way,

The one who died in the onerous criminal law he formulated himself was Han Fei.

Generals of Qin are Bai Qi and Wang Jian; the generals of Zhao are Lian Po and Li Mu,

Their expertise in wars and battles had proved so true.

The names and prestige of these generals went far to the

northern desert,

To remember them forever their reputation and portraits have got down to the historical record.

When harnessing flood Da Yu left his foot prints in all the nine regions,

The State of Qin annexed a hundred prefectures.

Mount Tai was the most prestigious among the Five Important Mountains,

Yunyunshan and Tingtingshan at the foot of Mount Tai were where the ceremony of offering sacrifice to the earth and heaven took place.

Yanmen is the famous pass on the northern frontier; the Great Wall is then called the purple fortress,

Jitian is the remotest point of official postal relay in the northwest regions,

Chicheng is a unique peak on the Tiantaishan.

To watch inland water one has to get to Dianchi Lake in Kunming; to view the sea one has to be at Jieshi Mountain,

Other lakes worthy of seeing are Juye in Shandong and in

Hunan Lake Dongting.

The land of China is so vast and infinite,

The high mountains and deep valleys are so majestic and grand.

D

The basic thing in running a country well is to develop agriculture,

A good job must be done in sowing and harvesting by the farmer.

A new round of farm work has been started on the sun-facing land,

What is to be sowed are corn and millet.

To submit freshly harvested grain as tax to the state,

According to their performance of farming farmers were awarded or punished and officials were promoted or deposed.

Meng Ke adored simplicity,

Shi Yu was upright and known for his honesty.

If one can act as the above two, he could almost be regarded as practicing the golden rule,

Diligence, modesty, caution and discreet are what they should also do.

When you listen to somebody, you have to examine if what he says was true and proper,

When you look at the appearance of others, you should tell if they have a good character.

The best thing to leave to the posterity is a piece of good advice,

Posterities should be asked to establish themselves and respect prudence.

Hearing derision and admonishment, examine thee,

Excessive affection may lead to the opposite way.

When insult and shame will fall on thee,

Retire from thine post and go into forest and lakes in the hills; thus thou keep troubles away.

The two Shus chose a right time to retire,

Nobody forced them to untie their official belts and take off their attire.

To live by oneself and pass days in leisure,

One can thus enjoy tranquility, without talking about who is right or wrong or better.

One can find pleasure in questing for ancient events and figures or read axioms and aphorism, and sitting pretty,

In doing so, one can get rid of all worries and be entirely idle and free.

Deliver things delightful and throw away boredom and encumbrance,

One can enjoy rapture and glee, having driven away annoyance.

The lotus in the pond is splendid and full of shine,

New sprouts are coming out of the grass and woods in the garden.

The loquat tree remains green even in winter,

The Chinese parasol tree withers as soon as autumn is near.

The old tree roots are long and wriggling,

The falling leaves in the air are fluttering.

The wandering crane is alone on its flight,

It was dashing up to the purple clouds high in the sky.

Being fully immersed in his studies in the noisy market shops,

What could catch Wang Chong's sight were only books and bookcases.

Be on guard against thoughtless remarks,

Beware of the eavesdroppers, even if there are no others.

Our food includes meat and grain,

They should be tasty and save people from food deprivation.

When one is full, slaughter a chicken or cooking a fish would seem redundant,

When one is hungry, husks and chaff would taste delicious.

Relatives are to be treated with warmth,

Food prepared for the old and the young should be different from yours.

Women should do a good job in domestic chores,

With great care to wait on their husbands.

The girl's round fan made of white silk is kept clean,

The silver white candle is bright and brilliant in the even.

A nap in the day and a sound sleep at night,
On the soft bamboo mat and ivory-decorated bed.
A banquet amid singing and dancing,
Officials are raising cups to drink for the feasting.

People wave their hands in rhythm and stamp the beat with their foot,
They are indeed joyful, peaceful and healthy and pleasant.
To carry on the family line from generations to generations,
Great care is needed when offering sacrifices in the four seasons.

To bow once and again, one should kneel down and touch the ground with one's forehead,
One should also be deferential when doing the offering.
Letters to others should be concise,
Prudence and details are needed when answering others' questions.

Take a shower after you have made yourself dirty,
You wish the hot weather could be cooled down when you can hardly put up with the heat.
Donkeys, mules, calves and cows are not good at running, yet they leap higher than horses when being terrified.

Bandits and thieves must be seriously punished,

Rebels and ruffians must be captured by the government.

Lü Bu was good at archery and Xiong Yiliao was a master of slingshot,

Ji Kang was known for his lute playing and Ruan Ji was able to give a long shout.

Meng Tian invented the brush pen while Cai Lun invented paper,

Ma Jun invented waterwheel and Mr. Ren was famous for fishing things so big that nothing can compare.

The skills and techniques of these people could either dissolve disputes or bring good to the society,

They have won warm acclaim from the people in the country.

Both Mao Qiang and Xi Shi had beautiful looks,

They looked pretty even when they frown and they had charming smiles.

Youth can be gone very quickly and time always tries to age people,

Only the sun can shine in the sky as long as possible.

The ladle of the Big Dipper changes its direction in each season,

The moon casts its light to all corners of the world while it is in motion.

When wood burns, fire can last, to pass on the kindling, one should cultivate himself and accumulate his happiness,

How nice it would be for posterities to enjoy a stable and peaceful life always.

To stride away with firm steps,

As of attending a ceremony in the temple, one should be serious and cautious.

One should be neatly dressed and look solemn,

One should also be cautious and prudent, and look far ahead with a high aim.

My knowledge is so limited and my information about the world is so superficial,

My foolish self is waiting for others to question and laugh at me for being shallow.

All I know are some auxiliary words,

Such as "to, of, oh and wow".

The *Verse* and Chinese Calligraphy
《千字文》与中国书法

Ever since the *Verse* came into being, it had served as one important subject matter of Chinese calligraphy. Many pieces of calligraphy that copied the *Verse* became master pieces. The *Verse* enhanced the development of calligraphy, and in return the calligraphy pieces greatly popularized the *Verse*.

自《千字文》问世后,它就成为中国书法重要的书写内容。很多书写《千字文》的书法成为杰作。《千字文》促进了书法的发展;反过来,书法也推广了《千字文》。

Calligraphy is a unique art form in China. It uses a pointed brush pen to write on rice paper in black ink. The earliest form of the calligraphy was inscriptions on oracle bones, and inscriptions on bronze and stone wares. In the Qin Dynasty the seal script was widely popularized, and clerical script appeared in the Han Dynasty; regular, freehand and cursive scripts appeared in the later periods.

书法是中国独一无二的一种艺术形式。它使用带尖的毛笔,蘸着墨在宣纸上书写。书法最早的形式是甲骨文和金文。到了秦朝普遍使用小篆,隶书出现在汉朝,在汉以后的年代里出现了楷书、行书和草书。

Chinese calligraphy has been reputed as "music without sound," as a sister of dancing since its horizontal, vertical, left and right strokes also dance on paper. Shen Yinmo (沈尹默, 1883-1971), the famous poet and calligrapher, remarked on calligraphy thus, "People have all recognized that calligraphy is the highest form of art, because it works wonders, it is so refreshing and pleasing to the eye that it produces a splendid picture without colors, and it gives out symphonic music without sound."

中国书法被誉为"无声的音乐",由于其横画、竖画、左右画在纸上舞动,也被视为舞蹈的姐妹。著名诗人和书法家沈尹默(1883—1971)说:"人们普遍认为书法是艺术的最高形式,因为它很神奇,给人以新鲜感,很养眼。它不使用颜色,却绘出了堂皇的画面;没有声音,却奏出了交响乐。"

The most important and influential calligrapher in Chinese history is Wang Xizhi (王羲之, 303-361) in the Jin Dynasty. He has been regarded a saint of Chinese calligraphy, and his *Prelude to the Orchid Pavilion* has been a model for all calligraphy learners in China. The *Verse* was not in existence at his life time, so he didn't write it. However, his grandson in the 7th generation, Monk Zhiyong (智永), whose original name was Wang Faji (王法极) honestly inherited and developed his calligraphy. His exact dates of birth and death are not available. He lived in the Southern Dynasty and the Sui Dynasty, and some said that he lived for over a hundred years.

中国历史上最重要、最有影响的书法家是晋朝的王羲之(303—361),他被誉为"书圣",他的《兰亭序》一直是所有学习书法的人临摹的样本。在他生活的年代,《千字文》尚未问世,因此在他的书法作品中没有《千字文》。然而,其七世孙,原名叫王法极的智永和尚忠实地继承并发展了他的书法艺术。智永和尚出生和去世的日期已无从查找,我们知道他生活在南朝和隋朝,有人说他活了100多岁。

The most remarkable thing is that Monk Zhiyong once wrote over 800 copies of the *Verse* in the "regular-cursive" script and widely distributed it. According to the *Periodical of Chinese Arts* (《中国艺术》), there are still two existing copies of this piece of calligraphy: one is in Japan (brought there in the Tang Dynasty), and the other is the copy printed by Xue Sichang (薛嗣昌) from a stone tablet in the Northern Song Dynasty, which has been collected in the "Forest of Stone Steles" in Xi'an.

相传智永和尚一生所做的最突出的事情是,他以真草书写过 800 多份《千字文》，并且广为散发。据《中国艺术》所载，目前存世的智永《千字文》尚有两件。一件在日本（唐朝时被带入日本）；另一件是北宋薛嗣昌石刻印本，现收藏在西安碑林。

According to the *Book Registered in the Years* 1119 – 1125 (《宣和书谱》) at the Imperial Court of the Northern Song Dynasty, there were 23 model calligraphy by Monk Zhiyong being registered, among which 15 were his calligraphy of the *Verse* in different scripts.

北宋朝廷的《宣和书谱》记载当时御府收藏了智永和尚 23 种帖，其中《千字文》15 种。

The famous calligraphy researcher Xiong Bingming (熊秉明, 1922 – 2002) remarked "the calligraphy of the *Verse* by Monk Zhiyong was an important link during the inheritance of calligraphy" in the *Theoretic System of Chinese Calligraphy* (《中国书法理论体系》). Bao Shichen (包世臣, 1775 – 1855), the famous calligrapher of the Qing Dynasty told us in his book *Narration of Books* II (《述书下》), "To look at him from the vertical perspective and in inheriting, he (Zhiyong) carried on what Cai Yong, Zhong Yao and Wang Xizhi have achieved; in opening up the future, he handed his best to Yu Shinan and the rest of the first generation of Tang Dynasty calligraphers. From the horizontal perspective, he distributed his 800 copies of the *Verse* he wrote down to temples in the south, and by doing so he presented a model to calligraphy learners. The influence of such an action was recorded in various documents, for instance, Zhang Xu, Sun Guoting, Ouyang Xun, Chu Suiliang, Huai Su and others had taken his *Verse* as their models. It is obvious that many famous calligraphers of the Song, Yuan and Ming Dynasties had copied his *Verse* in their practice, therefore Monk Zhiyong is an important person in the teaching of calligraphy."

著名书法研究学者熊秉明（1922—2002）在《中国书法理论体系》一书中说："在书法传授继承上，《千字文》是重要的一环。"清朝著名书法家包世臣（1775—1855）在《述书下》中说："在承先上，他（智永）继承了蔡邕、钟繇、王羲之，在启后上，他把书法传给虞世南，启发了唐书法家的第一代人物，这是纵的方面。横的方面，他写过《千字文》800本散给江南诸寺，这些《千字文》显然是给人们，特别是抄经的僧徒做范本用的，对当时一定有相当大的影响，对后世影响则是有据可查的，张旭、孙过庭、欧阳询、褚遂良、怀素诸人都临过，宋元明书家也都临过，所以智永是在书法教学起过示范作用的重要人物。"

So, the *Verse* by Monk Zhiyong is a mile stone in the history of Chinese calligraphy. It has been regarded as the last inheritor of Wang Xizhi's calligraphy and the best epitome of previous calligraphy and it is also the opener of learning calligraphy from examples since the Sui and Tang Dynasties. Without the *Verse* by Monk Zhiyong, the lofty historic position of Wang Xizhi could not have been established and the way of learning calligraphy from examples would not have been started. The *Verse* as a primer for children has inspired huge creativeness of calligraphers and has become a long lasting complex in the calligraphy field in China, and therefore, many versions of the *Verse* in various scripts have become classics of calligraphy. The following are best representatives of such classics.

所以,智永《千字文》在书史上是一个里程碑。它是王羲之书法在南朝的最后传承与集成者,也是隋唐帖学笔法的开启者。如果没有智永《千字文》,初唐将会难以认识与确立王羲之的书史地位,也无从开启初唐帖学笔法之源。《千字文》这样一本启童蒙的韵文激发了书法家巨大的创作力,在书法界构成了一种绵历久远的《千字文》情结,而且《千字文》创作也成为书史上产生经典最多的文本。下面是这些经典中最有代表性的几幅作品。

The first one we wish to mention is the *Verse* in regular script produced by Yan Zhenqing（颜真卿，709－784）. He was born in today's Xi'an. When he was practicing calligraphy in his childhood, his family was too poor to afford ink and paper! He used water mixed with yellow soil as his ink and practiced writing on walls. He was appointed an official after he scored high in the nation-wide imperial examination in 734. He was conferred Duke of Lu Prefecture.

我们首先要提到的是颜真卿（709—784）所书的楷书《千字文》。颜真卿出生在今日的西安。小时候家里穷，买不起墨和纸，就用水和着黄土，用笔蘸着在墙上练字。734年，他中了进士，开始做官，被封为鲁郡公。

Yan's regular script marked an important milestone in the history of Chinese calligraphy. His regular script stands as a school of his own and has been known as square in the shape, serious, upright and grand in its image. Some say the style of his calligraphy, an epitome of his personal character, did reflect the demeanor of the Tang Empire.

颜真卿的楷书是中国书法史上的重要里程碑，自成一体，方严正大。有人说他的书法风格是他的人格的缩影，而且特别体现了大唐帝国的风度。

It has been widely accepted that his regular script looks like a loyal official or a martyr. It may seem a bit awesome at the first glance, yet, it becomes affectionate if you view it for a long time and you would never be fed up with it. The dots seem to be falling stones; the horizontal lines are like clouds in the summer sky, and the vertical hooks are powerful.

大家公认他的楷书如忠臣烈士，人初见而畏之，然观愈久而愈觉可爱。其见宝于世者有必多，然虽多而不厌也。点如坠石，画如夏云，竖钩很有力。

The next one we want to mention is the work by Emperor Huizong of Song. His name is Zhao Ji（赵佶），and he was born in 1082 and died in 1135 at the age of 54. He was the 8th emperor of the Song Dynasty. He made extraordinary contributions to Chinese culture and art, as he formed his own style of regular script in calligraphy, which is called the "Golden Slender Script". The flowers and birds he painted were unique and also exquisite.

But historians didn't like him, they said that he was capable in everything, but not as an emperor. He was captured by the invading Jin troops and tortured to death.

下面我们要提到的是宋徽宗的作品。宋徽宗名赵佶，1082年出生，1135年54岁时去世。他是北宋第8位皇帝。他对中国的文化和艺术作出了卓越的贡献，他自创了书法楷书中的"瘦金体"，其花鸟画不但独特，而且精致。但是历史学家不喜欢他，说他诸事皆能，独不能为君。他最后被入侵的金兵所擒，备受折磨而死。

The *Verse* was written with a cursive hand in 1122. The characters in the piece seem to be forging ahead with ups and downs and also with some kind of rhythm; there is no trace of stagnation of the strokes, and it projects magnificent impression to viewers. It has been collected by Liaoning Provincial Museum and been regarded as one of the treasures of China. It is 11.72 meters in length and 0.315 meters in width. The paper is made of hemp with patterns of golden clouds and dragon and it is in a whole piece by a special technique. Much to our regret, the technique has been lost.

1122年，他用草书书写了《千字文》。其笔势奔放流畅，跌宕起伏，富有韵律，没有丝毫的涩滞，气势颇为壮观。此作品现被辽宁省博物馆收藏。作品写在整张描金云龙底纹白麻纸上，横长 11.72 米，纵长 0.315 米。这种纸张由特殊的工艺制成。遗憾的是，这种工艺已经失传。

The cursive hand style came into being in the beginning of the Han Dynasty. As a matter of fact, its name in the Chinese character is "草", which means "grass". This character can fully resemble the feature of this script—the strokes seem like dragons flying and phoenixes dancing. With such a style, one can write faster, with fewer strokes and in simpler structures; in such a style, radicals are replaced with dots or vertical lines; with such a style, one stroke can be connected with the other and a character can connect with another, and this is a better way to express the feelings of the calligrapher. Please do not think this is the easiest way of writing characters, on the contrary, it might be the most difficult way of writing, for instance, when you write a horizontal line, a longer line is a word and a shorter line may become another character.

草书始于汉初。其实它在汉语里用花草的草字为名。草字也反映了此书体之笔画龙飞凤舞的特点。用此字体书写笔画省略，结构简便。此字体以点画为基本符号来代替偏旁，是最具有符号化特征的书体；草书的笔画之间、字与字之间相互连带呼应，是便于快捷书写和便于表达书者情感的书体。不要以为草书是最好写的。其实，它最难写。譬如，一个横画若写得长一点或短一点，都可能变成另一个字。

Finally, let's come to the piece written by Qian Yong. He was born in a rich family in today's Wuxi. All his life he never attempted to sit for the imperial examination, therefore, he had never been an official. He was well versed in poetry, seal-carving and the clerical script of calligraphy. One interesting thing he did was that he proved, after thumbing through historical books, that the Chinese women have started foot-binding since the Southern Tang period, which existed in 937 - 975, rather than the Song Dynasty, as most people so believed. He left behind him many calligraphy works and many of them are still available.

最后，我们来看一看钱泳的作品。钱泳出生在今无锡一个富足的家庭里。他终生未参加过科举考试，因此从未当过官。钱泳工诗词、篆刻和隶书。他做过的一件有意思的事情是，他考证出中国妇女裹足自南唐（937—975年）开始，而不是很多人以为的始于宋朝。他身后留下了很多墨宝，有些到今天依然可以看得到。

His piece of the *Verse* was done in clerical script in the 10th year during the reign of Emperor Jiaqing, which is 1805. Clerical script evolved from the seal script and it is simpler than the seal script. It is not as tall as the regular script. Its horizontal stroke is the main feature, as it starts as the head of a silkworm and finishes as the tail of a swallow.

钱泳的《千字文》是他在嘉庆十年，即1805年时用隶书写的。隶书从篆书演变而来，比篆书要简单。隶书的字体比楷书要扁。隶书的横画讲究蚕头燕尾。

The strokes in this piece are neatly and orderly done. The characters look serious, but at the same time pretty. When a character has more strokes, the strokes are thinner, yet such a character arrays well with others. Some characters look like dancing girls. Some look like young handsome scholars. Some look like smiling old men and some look like kind old aunts. Often the stroke that goes to the lower right direction is wider, yet, it does not look ugly. The thinner verticals fit well with stout horizontals. His works have been used as a sample for learners to imitate.

钱泳的隶书《千字文》笔画工整，字体端庄秀丽。笔画多的时候，笔笔都较细瘦，与其他字很般配。有的像舞女，有的像年轻俊朗的书生，有的像微笑的老头，有的像慈祥的老姨妈。其字捺笔宽重，却不失美色；细竖画与粗横画相宜相依。他的作品常被用来临摹。

图书在版编目（CIP）数据

千字文：双语版：汉英对照/王荣华译注．－－北京：中国人民大学出版社，2022.10
ISBN 978-7-300-30854-8

Ⅰ.①千… Ⅱ.①王… Ⅲ.①古汉语-启蒙读物-汉、英 Ⅳ.①H194.1

中国版本图书馆 CIP 数据核字（2022）第 130611 号

千字文：双语版
王荣华　译注
Qianziwen

出版发行	中国人民大学出版社		
社　　址	北京中关村大街 31 号	邮政编码　100080	
电　　话	010－62511242（总编室）	010－62511770（质管部）	
	010－82501766（邮购部）	010－62514148（门市部）	
	010－62515195（发行公司）	010－62515275（盗版举报）	
网　　址	http://www.crup.com.cn		
经　　销	新华书店		
印　　刷	涿州市星河印刷有限公司		
规　　格	148 mm×210 mm　32 开本	版　次	2022 年 10 月第 1 版
印　　张	5	印　次	2022 年 10 月第 1 次印刷
字　　数	88 000	定　价	32.00 元

版权所有　　侵权必究　　印装差错　　负责调换